Richard Rubin

Living the Leopolds' Mi Casita Ecology

With a Foreword by Curt Meine
Photographs curated by Annette Rubin

The authors dedicate the proceeds of this book
to the nonprofit Taos Community Foundation

Friends of Mi Casita Fund

*for Leopold house preservation and
ecological inspiration.*

Image Credits:
p. iv. Excerpted from the Official Highway Map of New Mexico, prepared and issued by the New Mexico Department of Transportation. https://www.dot.nm.gov/travel-information/maps/

Back cover photo by Skip Belyea.
All other photos are by Richard and Annette Rubin

ISBN: 978-1-7378109-4-0
Library of Congress Control Number: 2022942480

Book and cover design by Anne Flanagan (adfbooks@mac.com)
Published by Nighthawk Press, P.O. Box 1222, Taos, New Mexico. 87571.
www.nighthawkpress.com
Printed in the United States of America.

NIGHTHAWK PRESS
TAOS, NEW MEXICO

Contents

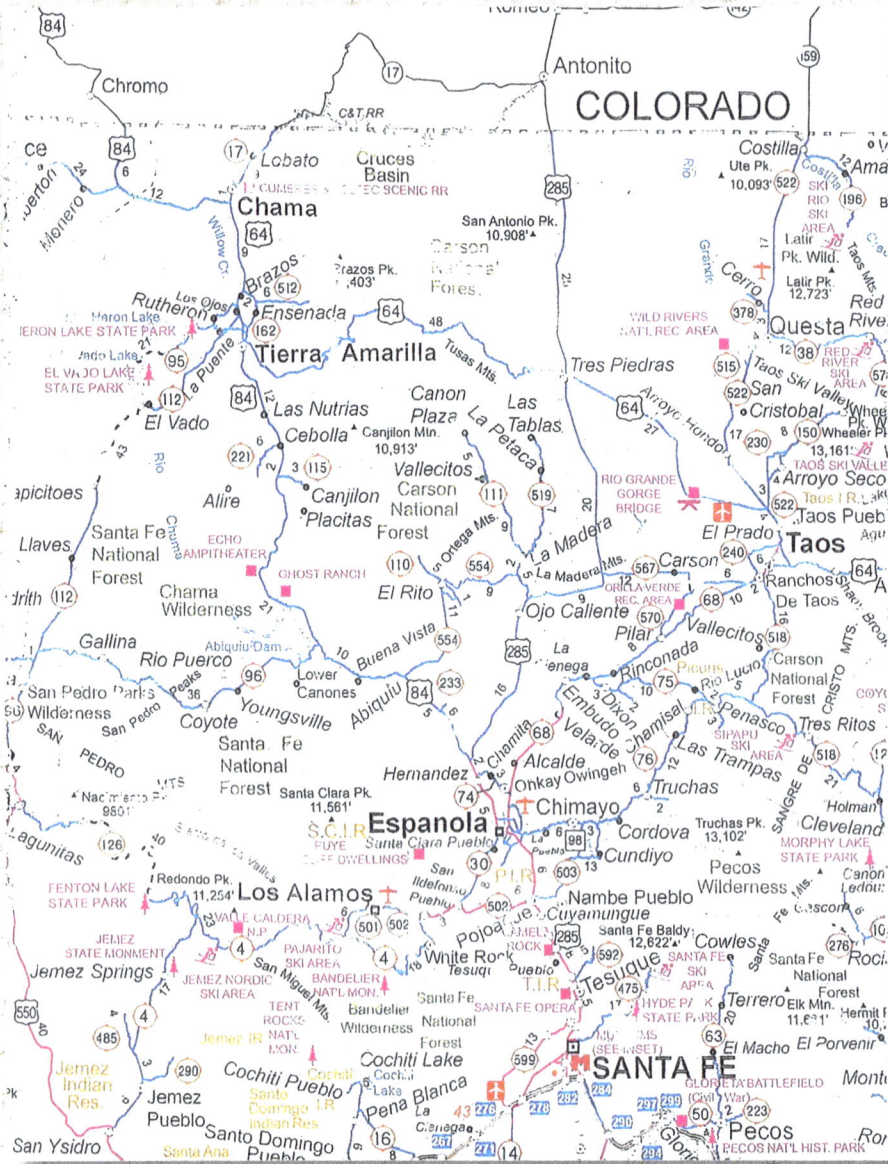

COLORADO

Chromo
Antonito
84
17
159

C&T RR

Cruces
Basin
Lobato
17
285
84
6
Ute Pk.
10,093'
Costilla
522
196
Ama

Chama
 CUMBRES & TOLTEC SCENIC RR
64
San Antonio Pk.
10,908'
Carson
National
Fores.
Cerro
RIO
SKI
AREA
Latir
Pk. Wild.
Latir Pk.
12,723'
378
Red
River
Questa

Los Ojos
Rutheron
Ensenada
512
6
Brazos Pk.
,403'
Brazos
162
HERON LAKE STATE PARK
Heron Lake
64
Tres Piedras
48
Tusas Mts.
Taos Ski Valley
515
San
Cristobal
Wheeler Pk.
13,161'
TAOS SKI VALLEY
Taos I.R.
Arroyo Seco
Taos Pueb
522
El Prado
Taos
Ranchos
De Taos

Tierra Amarilla
95
Vado Lake
EL VADO LAKE
STATE PARK
112
La Puente
84
Las Nutrias
Cebolla
Canjilon Mtn.
10,913'
Canon
Plaza
Las
Tablas
La Petaca
64
Arroyo Hondo
27
230
38
522
150 Wheeler Pk.
Agu

El Vado
221
115
3
Alire
Canjilon
Placitas
Carson
National
Forest
111
519
La Madera
567
240
567
Carson
568
10

Llaves
ECHO
AMPITHEATER
GHOST RANCH
Santa Fe
National
Forest
110
554
La Madera Mts.
ORILLA VERDE
REC. AREA
570
Pilar
Ojo Caliente
Vallecitos
518
Carson
National
Forest

drith
112
Chama
Wilderness
El Rito
Buena Vista
554
285
La
Cienega
Rinconada
Dixon
75
Picuris
Rio Lucio
Carson
National
Forest
COYO

Gallina
Abiquiu Dam
Lower
Canones
Abiquiu
84
233
Chamita
Embudo
Velarde
68
Chamisal
Penasco
SIPAPU
SKI
AREA
518
Tres Ritos
12

Rio Puerco
San Pedro Parks
Wilderness
96
Youngsville
Coyote
Santa Fe
National
Forest
Santa Clara Pk.
11,561'
Hernandez
74
Alcalde
Onkay Owingeh
76
Las Trampas

Nacimiento Pk.
9801'
S. ANTO...LOS VALLES
FUYE
CLIFF DWELLINGS
Espanola
Santa Clara Pueblo
La
Chimayo
98
Truchas Pk.
13,102'
Holman
Cleveland
MORPHY LAKE
STATE PARK

agunitas
126
Redondo Pk.
11,254'
30
San
Ildefonso
Pueblo
13
Cordova
Cundiyo
503
Pecos
Wilderness
Canon
Ledou

FENTON LAKE
STATE PARK
Los Alamos
501
502
P.I.R
502
Nambe Pueblo
Cuyamungue
285
Santa Fe Baldy
12,622'
Cowles
Santa Fe
National
Forest
276

JEMEZ
STATE MONMENT
VALLE CALDERA
N.P.
PAJARITO
SKI AREA
San Miguel Mts.
BANDELIER
NAT'L MON.
4
White Rock
Tesuqi
Pojoaque
NAMBE
ROCK
Pueblo
592
Tesuque
SANTA FE
SKI
AREA
475
Santa Fe
National
Forest
Roci

Jemez Springs
4
TENT
ROCKS
Bandelier
Wilderness
T.I.R.
Santa Fe
National
SANTA FE OPERA
HYDE PARK
STATE PARK
Terrero
Elk Mtn.
11,631'
Hermit Pk.

550
290
485
4
JEMEZ NORDIC
SKI AREA
Cochiti
N.T.
MON.
Cochiti Pueblo
Cochiti Lake
Cochiti
Lake
Cochiti I.R.
599
MUS EMS
(SEE INSET)
63
El Macho
El Porvenir
Mont

Jemez
Indian
Res.
Jemez
Pueblo
Santo
Domingo I.R.
Indian Res
Pena Blanca
La
Cienega
43
276
278
282
284
GLORIETA BATTLEFIELD
(Civil War)
297
299
50
2
223
Pecos

San Ysidro
Santo Domingo
Pueblo
Santa Ana
16
257
271
14
290
294
Glorie
PECOS NAT'L HIST. PARK
Ro

Foreword

In April of 1985, I found myself driving west out of Taos, New Mexico, crossing the wide basin of the upper Rio Grande, through vast sagebrush flats and over the deeply incised river gorge. I fixed my eyes on the horizon, looking for a pine-dotted outcropping of "three stones," sheltering a 73-year-old rustic bungalow. This was foreign territory to Midwestern me, and I reveled in its vistas. "Much grander and more distinctive than I'd pictured," I recorded in my journal. The elevation rising toward Tres Piedras. The "formidable" Sangre de Cristo Mountains to the east. The dark volcanic shield of San Antonio Mountain— Bear Mountain to the native Tewa—to the north. It was "altogether more open than I thought…magnificent."

I did come to the place with a mental image, developed in the basement of the agricultural library at the University of Wisconsin in Madison. I had been living there for months, immersed in the archival collection of Aldo Leopold's papers. My notebooks were dense with information gleaned from letters, logbooks, and reports from Leopold's time as a young U.S. Forest Service Officer in the Arizona and New Mexico Territories.

Leopold, newly appointed as supervisor of the Carson National Forest, had the house at Tres Piedras built as living quarters. (At the cost, he quipped, of "six-hundred-and-fifty large round silver dollars, coin of the realm.") I'd seen his colorful sketch of *Mia Casita.* I'd read his descriptions of his vision for the house. Tucked in under the protruding granite, it was built to Leopold's specs: simple, compact, equipped with a great fireplace and a wide front porch affording a fine view of the Sangre de Cristos.

Most important, I was privy to the private correspondence between Aldo and his bride-to-be Maria Alvira Estella Bergere. He was besotted. Estella was growing steadily and strongly in her affection. They married in Santa Fe in 1912 and moved into the house amid the rocks. A near-fatal bout of kidney disease would soon sideline Aldo and cut short their time together there. But Mia Casita would symbolize their life partnership, which would endure for thirty-six years and carry far-reaching consequences for Americans' evolving relationship with land—and for our relationships with one another on the land. The land ethic, as much as their five accomplished children, was a product of the Leopold marriage.

My first visit to Tres Piedras was brief, just enough to gain a feel for the place. The house was then still being used as the ranger's quarters. The Carson Forest archaeologist at the time, John Young, was eager to nominate it as a National Historic Site, which was finally accomplished in 1991. But another fifteen years would pass before Ben Romero put his shoulder to the effort of restoring Mia Casita, honoring its history while infusing the structures with new mission and purpose. Shortly after the main restoration work was completed—but before the installation of dependable running water, heating, and internet service—I returned to Tres Piedras to spend three frigid January days and nights, pondering what this reincarnation of Mia Casita might hold for future residents and visitors.

Now, another fifteen years on, we don't need to speculate. Mia Casita has become home to a growing and diverse community of volunteers and visiting students, Forest Service workers and researchers, scholars and neighbors. Notably, it has become a grounding place for an expanding circle of writers-in-residence and other creative spirits under a partnership with the Albuquerque-based Leopold Writing Program.

Mia Casita, with its back against the big rocks, still opens its doors compellingly toward the Sangre de Cristos. But its vista now embraces a wider world rising to meet the challenge of rapid social and environmental change. "Something really difficult is on the way," the late Barry Lopez said in delivering the Writing Program's first annual Leopold Lecture in 2017. "If we are going to survive and thrive in whatever landscape the world offers us in the decades ahead, we must learn to speak respectfully to each other, to listen to each other, to take into consideration the fate of each other's children."

I first came into the landscape of Mia Casita naïve about its deep natural and human history, its diverse cultur-

al influences, and its potential for biocultural regeneration through creative commitment. Now, with *Living the
Leopolds' Mi Casita Ecology,* Richard Rubin has provided a welcome introduction and grounding for future visitors from near and far. He orients us to the place where
in 1912, a young forester and the daughter of a storied
family of New Mexico just happened to find themselves
embarking on a new life together. Under the three rocks,
overlooking the upper Rio Grande Valley, they made their
first home. It has become a home again, for another generation carrying urgent hopes and visions.

Curt Meine
Senior Fellow
Aldo Leopold Foundation *and*
Center for Humans and Nature

Prologue

As a U.S. Forest Service seasonal and "newborn" to the agency in the early 1990s, I was introduced to Aldo Leopold as one of the originators of the concept of Wilderness, the big "W" that first came to fruition in the form of the Gila Wilderness on the Gila National Forest in 1924, before the Wilderness Act of 1964 was signed by Lyndon B. Johnson (after 8 years and 66 revisions). Today the Aldo Leopold Wilderness lies adjacent to its east.

The deeper dive came when I finally read *A Sand County Almanac* as part of a Wilderness and the American Ethic course at the Colorado Mountain College. This is where Mr. Leopold really got his hooks into me; here was a man who could evolve, change his mind, have wolf-killing regrets and encourage Americans to leave more and take less. From the position of seasonal archaeologist, I climbed the ladder to district and then Forest archaeologist in Colorado, often tasked with the preservation of historic buildings on National Forest System land. In 2006 I learned that *HistoriCorps,* a burgeoning nonprofit fueled by volunteers, was restoring the Aldo Leopold House (Mi Casita) on the Tres Piedras Ranger District of the Carson National Forest. I went on to work with HistoriCorps on several historic preservation projects before stepping foot in the hallowed bungalow tucked deep in the rocks for which Tres Piedras is known.

A man ahead of his time, Leopold designed the house to capture sun and take advantage of the thermal mass afforded by the rocks. It is also well situated to view spectacular rises of both sun and moon over the Sangre de Cristo range to the east. Aldo knew *feng shui* even if he did not know of the formal practice. But he wasn't alone; another hero of mine, Walter Perry, an early district ranger on the Carson, helped Leopold build Mi Casita, and shaped the volcanic stones that make up its grand fireplace.

I am now a deputy district ranger on the West Zone of the Carson NF that includes the Aldo Leopold House. Amazingly, I am now tasked with continuing further upgrades to the house to fully open her doors to the American public who will be able to reserve the house and experience this sacred space. This opportunity feels both rewarding and terrifying. I approach the task with the conviction that it is only right for the American public to experience the place where Leopold likely formed some of his most important thoughts around the conservation ethic. Terrifying in that it is a precious gem that we hope and trust people will leave better then they found it. Even more than that, my hope is they take some inspiration from the house out into the world. Through our new mandate of Shared

Stewardship, we are able to open the house with the help of benefactors and partners in the form of Dr. Richard Rubin, the new Friends of Mi Casita volunteers, and the Taos Community Foundation.

The Forest Service as a land management agency is facing the greatest challenges of its existence. The Southwest in particular is on the bleeding edge of a hotter and dryer planet, long term drought, megafires, a dwindling spring run-off, and increasing recreation impacts. I often wonder if I invited Aldo and Walter to a podcast what they would say about the state of our land and rural communities. As an archaeologist I still think about the anthropology of land use and abuse. As a decision maker, I continue to draw on Mr. Leopold's land ethic and Mr. Perry's model of understanding local northern New Mexico communities to make sound land management decisions.

Angie Krall
West Zone Deputy District Ranger
Carson National Forest

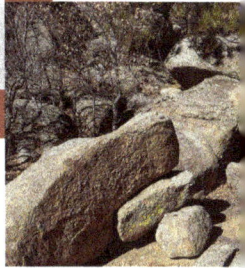

Preface

A modest cabin in Tres Piedras, New Mexico, is usually passed by travelers on Highway 285, a two-lane blacktop route that curves west from Espanola heading north to Colorado. A Forest Service notice indicates the entrance road is for "administrative purposes only." A large sign announces the phone number to adopt a wild horse, but the gate further is locked. This journal/guidebook will take you inside the life around this cabin from thousands of years ago and through the last century. The Craftsman bungalow was built in 1912 when Aldo Leopold was appointed Supervisor of the Carson National Forest. His new wife Maria Alvira Estella Bergere named it "my little house," *Mia Casita* in her formal Spanish. Much has been written about the Leopolds and we do not hope to approach others' scholarship. Rather, this blend of journal, discussions, and discursions tells stories about the human aspects of living and working in the Mi Casita rockscape.

The cabin and its community with the land and people are our main characters.

For readers interested in Aldo and Estella's lives, our stories will provide introduction to excellent biographic and critical references. That includes illustrative websites, such as the Wisconsin-based Leopold Foundation and the Albuquerque-based Leopold Writing Program. I have learned much serving as volunteer steward helping the U.S. Forest Service maintain Mi Casita over the past seven years. These stories will venture back to archaic, ancestral, and historic knowledge, then recognize the Leopolds' brief time here in Tres Piedras. Over the subsequent century to now, I will describe many human experiences around Mi Casita and consider their inspiration value about the problems challenging our living now in ecological community.

Our view combines attentive consciousness of the natural world and the valence of human life. Robin Wall Kimmerer states in *Kinship: Belonging in a World of Relations* (Volume 5, *Practice*):

> Paying attention, a compassionate kind of attention and empathic attention to the more-than-human world, seems a prerequisite for kinship and a practice that we have lost.

I learned years ago of anthropology "participant observation" study methods. I apply the term now to combine engagement and perceptive openness. The title term *ecology* emphasizes the relationship qualities of our perspective. The word was first coined in the late nineteenth century as a branch of biology dealing with the relations between organisms and their environment. Applications have since been expanded to the individual, population, community, ecosystem, and biosphere levels.

William Least Heat Moon in *Blue Highways* described "the civilizing influence of historical continuity." I start by leading you on the journey from our home in Arroyo Seco, New Mexico to Tres Piedras with this vision. Inspired by Least Heat Moon, U.S. Highway 64 is a Blue Highway on the New Mexico Department of Transportation map I found curled in my truck door pocket. In the Preface he tells us:

> On the old highway maps of America, the main routes were red and the back roads blue. Now even the colors are changing. But in those brevities just before dawn and a little after dusk— times neither day nor night—the old roads return to the sky some of its color. Then, in truth, they carry a mysterious cast of blue, and it's that time when the pull of the blue highway is strongest, when the open road is a beckoning, a strangeness, a place where a man can lose himself.

Our goal is to tell the stories about community convergence of the land, the people, the more-than-human life, the legacy of Aldo and Estella Leopold, continuing influence of their inspiration, and initiatives for ongoing preservation of these values. We illustrate these with many anecdotes about how diverse people and I myself engaged there. Our perspective comes from Aldo Leopold's definition in his essay "The Land Ethic," as published in the 1966 popular paperback edition of *A Sand County Almanac:*

> All ethics so far evolved rest upon a single premise: that the individual is a member of a community of interdependent parts. His instincts prompt him to compete for his place in that community, but his ethics prompt him also to co-operate (perhaps in order that there may be a place to compete for).
>
> The land ethic simply enlarges the boundaries of the community to include the soils, waters, plants, and animals, or collectively: the land (p. 239–240).

It is inconceivable to me that an ethical relation to land can exist without love, respect, and admiration for land, and a high regard for its value. By value, I of course mean something far broader than mere economic value; I mean value in the philosophical sense (p. 261).

Marcelo Gleiser, cosmology philosopher at Dartmouth College, asks in *Volume 1: Planet* of the *Kinship* series:

Religion comes from the Latin word for religio, which means "to reconnect." The question is, What religions are you reconnecting with? … Adam and Eve were very happy with God in paradise.… In my case, the reconnection is with the natural world itself.

Mi or Mia Casita

The cabin name presents a historical conundrum. Commonly called Mi Casita now, Curt Meine states in his thorough Leopold biography that "Estella and Aldo jointly agreed to call the house *Mia Casita*" (p. 120). He confirmed their ongoing use of this name recently in a personal communication. The memoir of Walter Perry, the cabin builder, calls it Mia Casita. All of the literature about this period in the Leopolds' lives uses the name Mia Casita. However, the pronoun *mia* is confounding. It does not appear in Ruben Cobos's *Dictionary of New Mexico Spanish.* My Castillian *Cassell's Spanish Dictionary* defines *mia* as "a contingent of Moroccan troops," clearly not the Leopolds' intent!

Local colloquial use favors Mi Casita. *Casita* is feminine, and *mi* has no specific gender in *Cassell's.* However, current online translation sources state that *mia casita* and *mi casita* both mean "my little house." I consulted a ninth generation Taos Norteño friend who is historical culture

House Setting

astute, Felipe Santisteban. He said *mia* doesn't fit local usage, usually meaning *mine,* and *mi* would be his vocabulary choice. He agreed with my interpretation that *mia* was more formal, fitting Estella's social strata, and *mi* would be more common parlance. I decided to recognize Estella's preference applying *mia* in this book for historic descriptions but use *mi* in our title and stories as an expression of quotidian community.

Acknowledgements

Richard is the primary narrator of this journal and Annette is curator of the photographs. We are grateful to the U.S. Forest Service staff for encouraging and enabling our engagement. The historic house, library, and furnishings are all property of the Forest Service and inclusion of their history in this book is authorized. The information described here was derived from the author's direct experience, public sources such as organization websites, and contributions by the named individuals. We thank the Leopold Writing Program for restoring literary vitality to Mi Casita and the Aldo Leopold Foundation in Wisconsin for ongoing education resources. During the drafting of this book, Courtney White and Curt Meine provided more works to benefit the Mi Casita library and my own education. And I particularly thank Angie Krall (West Zone Deputy District Ranger) and scholar Curt Meine for their powerful personal statements about our Mi Casita inspiration. We also thank Rebecca Lenzini of Nighthawk Press who provides the means for Taos authors to produce works contributing to our community. We hope that our telling of these stories will invigorate interest in the new Friends of Mi Casita initiative for preservation, public access, and contribution to environmental regeneration. The Friends of Mi Casita projects are supported by a non-profit Community Impact Fund under the sponsorship of the Taos Community Foundation

In telling stories of archaeology, history, and environmental science, we do not pretend to be rigorous academics, but rather offer accessible knowledge and opportunities. This small book is an addition to the authors' Taos Cultural Ecology Trilogy for craft, community, and philanthropy.

Richard Rubin

The Conscious Journey to Mi Casita

Well, it's a mighty world we live in, but the truth is, we're only passin' through. The local trio Rifters, in *The Great River* album.

From Home to Mi Casita

Annette and I built our home on the high plains at 7,200 feet just below the Carson National Forest El Salto Peak and Wheeler Peak Wilderness to the east. From our patio and garden, we look west across the sagebrush *llano* plain, over the Rio Grande Gorge towards small *cerro* volcano domes. The Gorge is defined as a geological *rift,* and we appreciate our local musicians' insight. On the U.S. Geological Survey topographic maps, the distance to Tres Piedras is twenty-five miles by the proverbial measure "as the crow flies." We live with many crows, significant homescape companions. Yet I observe their raucous activity is rarely straight lining. An online search reveals one origin of the phrase as the practice of ships carrying cages of crows before modern navigational instruments. A bird would be released to fly directly (it was hoped) towards land. Maybe "beeline" is more accurate ethology now. Nor are other avian neighbors good models. Magpies, the cousins of crows, are gregarious and smart, but I have not observed any west of the Rio Grande Gorge closer to Tres Piedras. Hawks are impressive, flying in high circles looking for prey. Sandhill cranes are associated with the Leopolds, breeding in the marshes near the Baraboo, Wisconsin "Shack" on their famous old farm restoration. The cranes winter in the central New Mexico Bosque del Apache Preserve. However, as I observe flocks flying high over Mi Casita, they follow a straight north–south route along the Tusas Mountains ridges, considered the southernmost extension of the Colorado San Juan Mountains. Forest Service Biologist Cheron Ferland identified their distinctive voices as *gurgling*.

By vehicle, I travel a different route there of thirty-four miles and, more important to this narrative, through many dimensions of observation and memory.

Leaving our home on the road away from Taos Ski Valley, we go through the turns of Arroyo Seco village. (For millennia of stories about people on this land, see our 2021 book *Homescape Rewilding*.) Tuning our perception to this drive, notice the signs indicating Taos Land Trust conservation easements. As we approach Arroyo Seco village with wetlands and pasture on our right, El Salto Road climbs the foothills to our left. Up a short way but private is the former home of esteemed author Frank Waters who deeded eight acres to become the first Taos Land Trust conservation easement. Past the funky village shops, galleries, and diverse eateries, we drive along a boundary of Taos Pueblo land. A resident redtail hawk often perches in a tall cottonwood, surveying these sagebrush and grass lands, fulfilling his role in the food chain. We watch for skunks who like the adjacent section of wetland, often waddling along the road at night.

Continuing south for a few miles on the blue highway, we come to a conventional looking four-way stoplight intersection. However, for the savvy, it is a portal into other times. About twenty-five years ago, the existing four-way stop signs and blinking traffic light were modernized. A good move for improved safety, but the blinking light intersection had been an important crossroads for route directions. We are coming from State Road 150, also known as the Ski Valley Road, on the east. Turning north leads to the village of Questa and eventually Colorado. A left turn south goes to the Town of Taos in several miles. Heading straight west is our route to the Rio Grande Gorge Bridge and Tres Piedras.

Given the importance of the blinking light as a landmark for directions, especially for visitors, the *Taos News* conducted a survey of what to call the new stoplight intersection. The community overwhelmingly voted for "Old Blinking Light" as the continuing name for this prominent guidepost. A nearby restaurant even changed its name from the Chile Connection to the Old Blinking Light. You could get a Euro sticker OBL. While a neat story, what is the ecological significance? For me, it begins a change in perspective, a shift in awareness opening to perceptions of tradition, nature, and culture on my frequent twenty-seven mile drive from the OBL intersection to Tres Piedras.

History and Ecology on the Road

In one hundred yards, Blueberry Hill Road starts on our left, heading to the south along a dry ridge above the irrigated bottomland of the area called Lower Los Colonias. When sponsoring an archaeological study of land at the Millicent Rogers Museum close by, I learned that numerous sites of ancient camps and pit houses have been discovered there. Evolving ideas about these previous human communities on the land are important for this journal of Mi Casita ecology. Understanding the reasons people developed these sites, the periods they occupied them, and the routes they travelled is changing. Scientific discoveries have expanded knowledge of the diversity and duration of these dynamics in the Southwest. Modern Pueblos have been recognized as built by migrating tribes seeking better climate for agriculture, hunting, and defense safety. For example, the November 26, 2021, issue of *Science* magazine describes study of sixth century volcanic eruptions in the Western hemisphere Arctic that forced Athabascan people to migrate south.

Human Influence

These human movements enabled the formation of larger social groups and farming of new crops. Native American political activists currently say they have been on the land since "time immemorial." But we need to recognize the diversity, competition, and at times hostility between many clan, language, racial, and tribal denominations. We also need to distinguish out of respect and understanding the difference between religious origin stories and evolving science. I compare this to my own culture's equal importance but fundamental differences between biblical creation stories and modern archaeology and historical science views.

Indigenous footprints were recently discovered at White Sands in southern New Mexico and dated to 23,000 years ago, prompting political controversy over historic entitlements. Taos Pueblo is a recent example of changing people on the land. A group from the Tewa tribe in the mid Rio Grande Valley moved north seeking better farming and hunting environments about eleven hundred years ago and gradually built the permanent structure we see today.

Culture and land conflicts continue. On our drive, you can see a small prayer stick with feathers on the south side of Route 64 at mile marker 248. This was left by the Native American and Anglo protesters of a deep well drilling authorized by the Abeyta Legal Settlement Agreement, reached in 2012. That agreement sought to settle a long-standing conflict between the El Prado Water District, the Taos Valley Acequia Association, Taos Pueblo, the Town of Taos, the State of New Mexico, and the United States Government as trustee for the Pueblo. Far more complicated than I can summarize here, the situation represents historic and continuing battles over water and land use authority and conservation. For our journey now, it is a reminder that although legally judged, protesters continue conscious of the struggle. Political revanchism is still intense between Native American activists and European "unsettlers," to use Wendell Berry's term.

Prairies and Forests

As we head west, smile at a pasture on the right where a handsome pinto burro grazes. Not alone, she has a brown

friend. Ascending the highway hill, a large standing wood-
man marks the Olguin Sawmill entrance. Run by former
Taos Mayor Dan Barrone and family, it is a business representing centuries of regional human relationship with
harvesting trees. Ecological issues range from the valuable utility of harvesting to exploitation. All local cultures
have benefitted from the trees to build shelters, fuel home
fires, and craft furniture, to mention a few end uses for
the cut trees. I value the availability at Olguin's of untreat-
ed natural boards for garden beds, stump rounds to support the soil weight of Annette's raised tomato bed, *latilla*
posts for protective fencing, and cedar for *horno* cooking.
The process of local forest harvesting is important in defining value, not necessarily exploitation. Trees are cut on
both private and public lands. Thinning reduces fire risks
from excessive density and is distinct from clear-cutting,
which increases erosion. An important focus for our journey is awareness of forestry's role in our ecology. The local cultures all live in relationship with the forests, whether Native American hunter, Norteño Hispanic farmer and
sheepherder, Anglo settler, modern outdoor recreator, or
contemporary environmental advocate. The nearby National Forest administration regulates the process and issues wood cutting permits for its public lands.

Forestry brought Aldo Leopold to the Southwest. When
President Teddy Roosevelt established the U.S. Forest Service, philanthropists endowed the first professional forestry school at Yale University. Raised in Burlington, Iowa,
where his immigrant grandfather helped establish a furniture factory and his father was an avid outdoorsman,
Aldo went east to Lawrenceville Prep School in New Jersey, and then entered the forestry program at Yale. In 1909

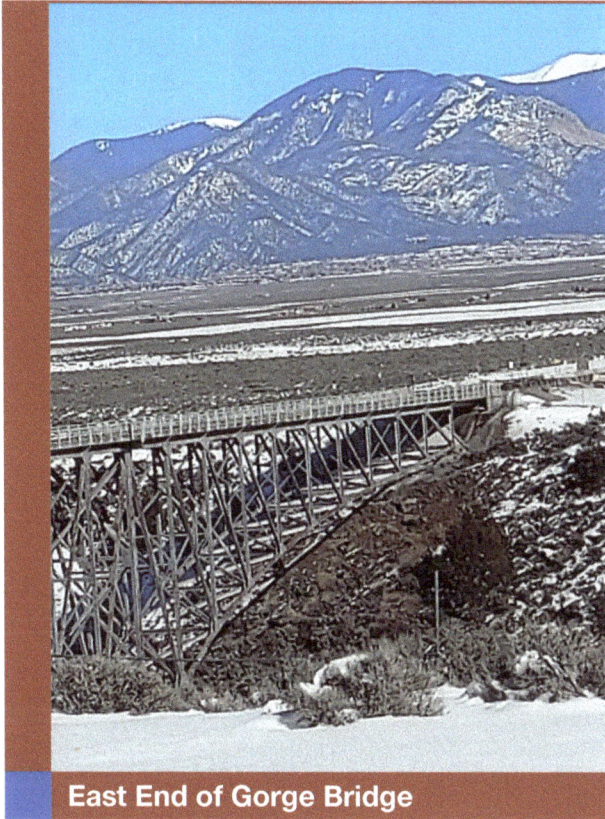

East End of Gorge Bridge

he was assigned to the Apache National Forest when Arizona was still a territory. Aldo was promoted in 1911 to Supervisor of the Carson National Forest. That's why our Mi Casita story leads to Tres Piedras.

The More Than Human Community

Approaching the Rio Grande Gorge Bridge, we can begin to see the home range of resident ungulates. I have sometimes observed six different large hooved mammals on a drive, and three more are there but elusive. These herds all have history in community with humans. The prairie along the gorge is a refugium for a flock of bighorn sheep. These natives became extinct here due to overhunting but were

Don't Fence Us In

Bighorn Refugium

restored about twenty years ago from Wyoming stock. More are flourishing in the Wheeler Peak Wilderness. But they still roam freely despite our fences. I have found grazers along the road near the Gorge bridge.

The bridge is six hundred feet above the river. The pedestrian walkways are a tourist attraction, very popular for taking selfies. Careful observation reveals blackish basalt rock below the brown granite walls. The bridge is over what is called the Lower Box of the Gorge. If you go further north, and hike down several trails into the Middle Box, as I did in the past when fly fishing at the confluence of the Red River and Rio Grande, you will find many slick black basalt rocks to maneuver. The newer, small *cerro* volcanoes had spread lava on the older granite. In addition to large basalt rocks, the entire area from Albuquerque north is abounding with whitish-gray volcanic rock leaving us a lithic archive. Also part of the Rio Grande del Norte National Monument, the Upper Box access is very rugged with extreme rapids during runoff season.

Creative Architecture and Land Stewardship

After crossing the bridge, you pass the Earthship Biotecture community on the right. According to its website, architect Michael Reynolds developed homes that people without specialized construction skills could build and that could be sustainable with indigenous and recycled materials, natural energy and water sources.

Across the highway from the Earthship Visitor Center, notice the gate for Wolf Springs Ranch which rises over the mesa on the volcanic plateau called La Otra Banda. My Norteño consultant Felipe Santisteban agrees this means

Range Restoration

"the other side," maybe relating to the Gorge when traveling from Taos. According to a video on the Taos Land Trust website, owner Tony Benson placed a significant chunk of his 3,450-acre ranch under conservation easement in 2003. For our ungulate tour, just past the ranch gate, notice a solar panel and tank maintaining a water supply for his herd of llamas and alpacas, our second and third ungulates.

Our journey's fourth is a group of black angus cows from the ranch. Small bands are moved in rotation which sustains the grass roots and usefully churns the soil surface for natural grass reseeding. This is a technique for more sustainable grazing management. The Land Trust description states that over one hundred years ago, the region was grassland in a piñon, juniper, and scrub oak savanna. That ecosystem was devastated by overgrazing in the late 1800s. The soil was blown away and sagebrush became dominant. Benson cleared dead piñon trees and thinned overgrown juniper in the higher elevation sections and that allowed sunlight and rain to nurture native grass seeds. Removing sagebrush and more grass seeding enabled healthy growth in the lower elevations. The diversity from blue grama and sand dropseed to squirrel tail and bunch grasses can better hold the natural water and bring back much wildlife. Spouse Martha told me a fire in 2008 cleared an area of scrub and allowed more grass recovery.

Notice the blue and silver heart shaped sculpture up the south hillside near mile marker 238. Tres Piedras sculptor and prior ranch hand Robert Unsor created it several years ago. He told me it is one piece of cottonwood with mosaic of mirrors. Robert wants it to be a message of community love.

We continue our westward drive looking for more ungulates and, after a few miles, we sight a large brown and white llama that likes to graze outside his fence close to the road. The herd is usually upslope a few hundred yards. Depending on the time of year, this range may include a couple dozen bison. Further along, more large black cattle spread about, but they look different with shaggy coats and long horns. Yes, a local rancher raises yaks. In addition, although my drives are always by day, road signs warn of elk and mule deer crossings, more likely at dusk and dawn. Last, I have not seen pronghorn, the shy small

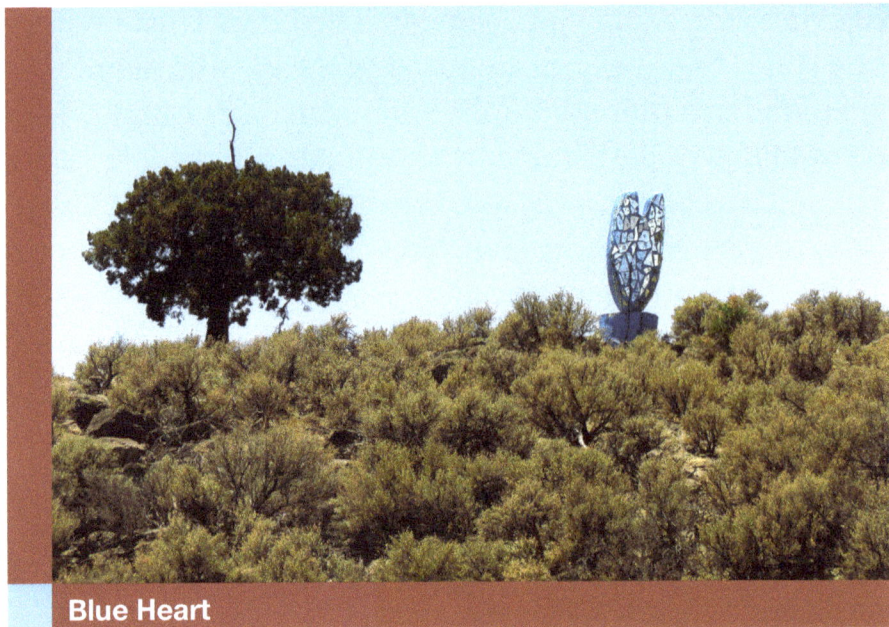

Blue Heart

antelope reported living up the higher ground on Wolf Springs Ranch. When we get further along the road west, San Antonio Mountain comes into view at two o'clock, situated about nineteen miles north of Tres Piedras. At 10,908 feet, it is the highest peak in the Taos Plateau volcanic field. Protected as a Wilderness Study Area, pronghorns survive wild there.

Dynamic Geology

Looking west from our home, the *cerro* volcano remnants are prominent, blocking the view to Tres Piedras. There are dozens of these small domes along the Rio Grande Gorge. Geologically called a *rift,* the Gorge was formed from the ancient granite crust when it split; it is different from deep canyons cut by wind and water through sandstone. Yes, that's the source of the name for the Rifters trio. As described in *Roadside Geology of New Mexico,* the rift splits the southern end of the Rockies into two prongs, the Sangre de Cristo Range, which includes the Taos Mountains on the east side and the Tusas and Brazos Mountains to the west.

Fourteen and a half miles from the Old Blinking Light, after Highway 64 has turned northwest, a sign points us east towards Cerro Montoso, Cerro de la Olla, and Cerro de Chiflo. *Montoso* means wooded land, *olla* means pot, and *chiflo* means flue or stovepipe according to Ruben Cobos's *A Dictionary of New Mexico and Southern Colorado Spanish.* Readers who know Castillian Spanish may find some words unfamiliar. The local Norteño dialect includes elements surviving from the seventeenth-century colonists. Be alert as these xeric lands often spawn *tornillo* dust devils.

This *cerro* biome is under Bureau of Land Management supervision as National Conservation Lands, part of the Rio Grande del Norte National Monument. Legislation has been proposed for Cerro de la Olla Federal Wilderness Area status. According to a *Taos News* report, keeping the mountain roadless protects it as a migratory passage for elk, bear, mountain lion, and other wildlife. Secretary of the Interior Deborah Haaland is quoted saying "Senator Ben Ray Lujan and I aim to ensure tribal, *acequia,* land grant and other communities can continue to practice their traditions and their environmental stewardship that have been passed down through generations."

Continuing on Route 64 west, we can see the northern Jemez Mountains to the south at ten o'clock. The town of Los Alamos overlooks the Bandelier National Monument. Taos author Frank Waters set his novel *The Woman at Otowi Crossing* where an old road down the mesa in Manhattan Project days borders San Ildefonso

Cerro Vista on the Blue Highway

Pueblo. This reminder of Waters contributes to our experience. His major literary theme is our profound and irrevo-
cable identity as part of each other and part of the whole,
as described in Thomas Lyon's Introduction to that book.
Looking south at eleven o'clock, we see Tres Orejas, a distinctive *cerro* that resembles coyote ears. In *New Mexico
Place Names,* T.M. Pearce states the Tewa name meaning
"coyote ear mountains" is *nday-oyay peeng-ya.*

A half mile before the Tres Piedras blinking light intersection, the highway crosses a wide arroyo. A large state sign
announces:

> Arroyo Aguaje Bridge: The pony truss bridge was built in 1934
> as a national recovery project. It has been preserved by the New
> Mexico State Highway and Transportation Department.

2

Our Shared Environment

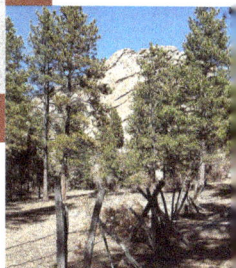

History of the Rocks

When our road descends from the Taos Plateau, the distinctive large rock monuments that define Tres Piedras appear. While the traditional name is translated as "three rocks," many other outcroppings of brown granite are visible in a wide view. However, I can see how the prominent three have been a travelers' landmark for millennia. Researching the history, our *Roadside Geology* guide describes that around 1.35 billion years ago, great masses of magma slowly cooled into reddish granite. Subsequent events are described in numerous geology texts. For today's view, the rosy color comes from feldspar minerals that have turned reddish due to bombardment by radioactive decay particles. Some of the granite is hardened by mineral substances leached to its surface by evaporation of moisture. Such rock erodes into especially odd shapes where the hardened surface has been broken. These are the large Tres Piedras rocks we encounter now as mythic.

Yes, mythic and mysterious. Northern New Mexico is an example of the worldwide "Great Unconformity" in geology lingo. This name refers to a gap in the geological record found in various locations around the world. Powerful ancient forces squeezed the land, building up mountain ranges and converting some sedimentary rocks to metamorphic varieties of granite and quartz. The northern part of New Mexico remained above sea level until about 720 to 635 million years ago when rising seas washed extensive erosion debris into the mantle at the junctions of crust plates. Where this is the case, as in the Sangre de Cristo mountains, the early sedimentary rock formations are missing. We live in a gap of missing time.

Modern Loci

At the junction of east-west Highway 64 and north-south 285, there is still a blinking light which roughly defines the center of Tres Piedras Village. The old gas station there has long been closed, but an active volunteer fire station is adjacent. A road sign directs a turn up Route 285 to the Cumbres and Toltec Railroad. That is not the historic Chili Line running through Tres Piedras—more on that later. The Cumbres and Toltec is a remnant of the narrow-gauge line that ran between Antonito, Colorado and Chama, New Mexico. It is now a fun scenic experience run seasonally.

We are now at approximately 8,000 feet elevation. Continuing west on 64, we enter the Carson National Forest. The sagebrush plain changes to ponderosa yellow pines

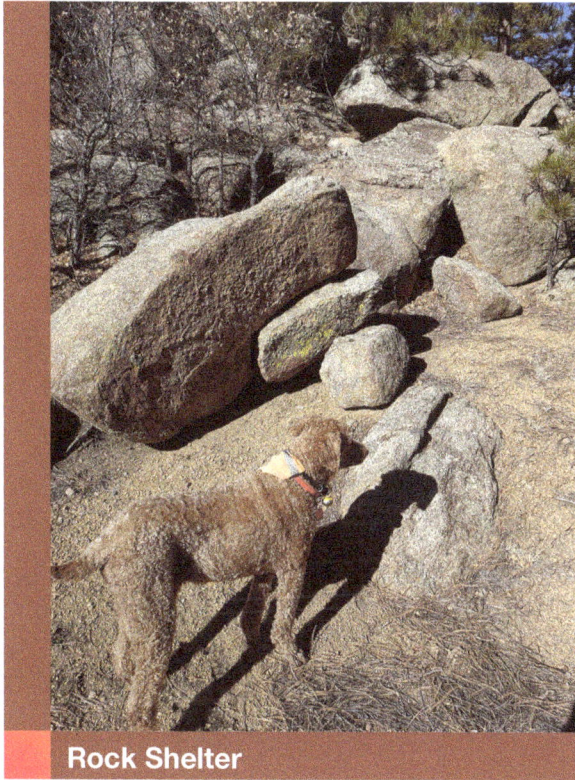
Rock Shelter

and Gambel oak chapparal. Our odyssey can reach back to the earliest maps from the 1770s which show the name Piedras de los Carneros, meaning Rocks of the Sheep, suggesting the habitat of bighorn sheep or pastoral grazing locations. Mi Casita was built against the middle rock. Signs and sightings of elk, mule deer, bobcats, and coyotes, as well as numerous birds and rodents, are common now. Mountain lions were occasional in the Leopold days. More on current wildlife observations later in this journal.

A 1987 article by Edwards et al., "Terrestrial Ecosystems Survey of the Carson National Forest," concluded that 168 environmental categories existed. Jeffrey Boyer's *Mu-*

seum of New Mexico 1990 Report of the Tres Piedras Ar-
chaeological Project states:

> These units characterize specific regions in terms of the interac-
> tion of climate, soils, and plant communities, and provide con-
> cise and informative descriptions of the natural environment.

The lower lands, including an area in front of Mi Casita
at the Carson Forest boundary, support piñon, scrub oak,
big sagebrush, juniper, and blue grama grass. Where water
collected, old cottonwoods grew.

Human Archaeology

Boyer states that this northern area is one of the least
studied in New Mexico, and only general background is
known for the prehistory and history of the region. In the
entire Taos Valley during the so-called Paleo-Indian Period circa 10,000 to 6,000 B.C.E., scattered artifact fragments
have been found. In the Archaic Period from 6,000 B.C.E. to
1,100 C.E., features of an Upper Rio Grande culture have
been recognized in the area from Tres Piedras north to
San Antonio Mountain that preceded larger Puebloan oc-
cupation to the east. These included campsites, workshops
for producing tools, defensive lookouts, and rock shelters.
However, none of the sites reflect the development of a
sedentary lifestyle; all have been primarily hunting and
gathering locations. The report about Tres Piedras from
the New Mexico Office of Archaeological Studies website,
a division of the New Mexico Department of Cultural Affairs, confirms that the sites represented a broad range of
temporal and ethnic affiliations: mobile hunter and gath-
erer groups during the Middle and Late Archaic periods
(1,800 B.C.E–600 C.E.); Jicarilla Apaches during the Mexican and American Territorial periods (1821–1912); and

Tres Orejas and Pedernal

Native, Hispanic, and Anglo use of the area during the New Mexico Statehood period (1912–present).

Boyer goes on to say that the presence of Puebloan Natives in the western area of Taos Valley remains largely unknown and is only suggested by pot sherds in a few sites. Of various types, it is not possible to determine if they are Puebloan or Apache, but they were likely used in transient forager base camps. Similarly, lithic scatter sites from tool and point making are not diagnostic of the makers or ages. Common stone artifacts include Polvadera obsidian from nearby Rio Arriba County and Pedernal chert from the Jemez Mountains and Abiquiu area. *Polvadera* in Spanish means *dusty* and *pedernal* means *flint*. An ancient mine is on the north side of this small butte made iconic in the paintings of Georgia O'Keefe.

Later, in the so-called Historic Period, Plains Native American groups are evident in the archaeological record and early Spanish documents. By the late fifteenth century, trade interactions were frequent among the Puebloans, Apaches, Kiowas, and Utes. In the eighteenth century, Jicarilla Apaches were driven westward from the Cimarron area by Comanche attacks, leaving sherd evidence near Tres Piedras. The present Jicarilla Reservation is nearby to the northwest across the Tusas Mountains. Among the most interesting nineteenth- and early twentieth-century artifacts recorded by Boyer is a soldered can perforated with a square nail. Apaches used these to brew *tiswin,* a form of corn beer.

On a recent tour of the Mi Casita rocks with Forest Service Archaeologist Price Heinl, we found numerous lithic scatter pieces. The rock formations close to Mi Casita show many sites useful for weather and enemy protection. We also found more recent artifact fragments of purple glass predating restriction of manganese use by the military in World War I. These should be distinguished from subsequent brown beer bottle pieces. Such archaeologic sites are so numerous around Mi Casita that plans to build a public hiking trail were altered for necessary protection.

Settlement in the seventeenth and eighteenth centuries by Hispanic people brought significant changes in culture, economics, and land use. New domestic animals and plant foods were developed in both subsistence homesteads and commercial pastoralism. The northwestern valleys were valuable for sheepherders of large flocks, often controlled by southern New Spain land grant owners. As markets increased in California and Colorado in the nineteenth century, these commercial flocks became a major source of income. More pressure for land grazing access came with expansion of Texan cattle ranching. This history is extensively described in Andrew Gulliford's 2018 *The Woolly West*. Besides Norteño sheepherders, Basque, Greek, and later Peruvian workers left cultural remnants in this region. Other European, *Tejano*, and Mormon settlers brought more diversity to the Tres Piedras area. After the Mexican American War and subsequent greater safety from the U.S. Army presence, the town of Tres Piedras was officially founded in 1879, but has never been incorporated.

Remembering the Chili Line

In the late nineteenth and early twentieth centuries, logging, railroads, and mining substantially changed the environment. The crucial development was the Denver and Rio Grande Western narrow-gauge railroad, known as the Chili Line. In 1880, the D&RG and the Atchison, Topeka & Santa Fe began extending the line from Antonito, Colorado south. Originally allowed as far as Espanola, purchase of an additional small line enabled it to reach Santa Fe by 1908. It then ran daily between Antonito and Santa Fe.

According to Mike Butler in *Tracking the Chili Line to Santa Fe,* Aldo Leopold was first stationed on the Carson at Antonito in May, 1911. But when promoted to supervisor in 1912, he moved the headquarters to Tres Piedras, more central in the Forest. Butler suggests Leopold also wanted proximity to new love Estella, often riding the Chili Line for visits to Santa Fe. Leopold described it as "slower'n a burro and just as sorry" (43). They were later married in October 1912.

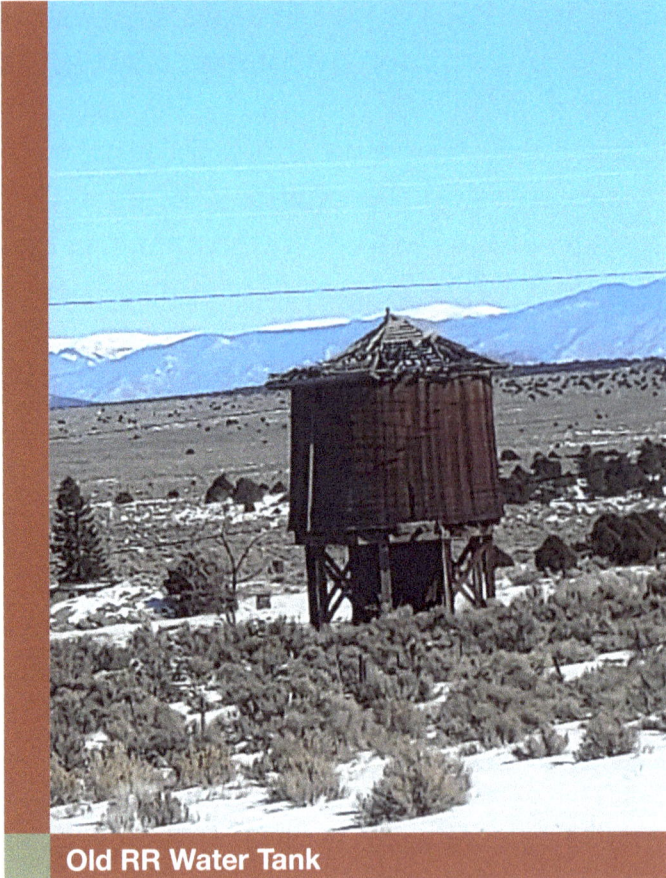

Old RR Water Tank

As I study the evolution of land and human culture around Tres Piedras, I find that the railroad fostered expansion of commercial enterprises. The mixed trains carried freight, mail, and passengers. Sheepherders and lumbering operators could move animals and products among local villages and connect with larger rail hubs. Stations and villages developed along the line, including Tres Piedras, Servilleta, Caliente, Palmilla, Volcano, Skarda, No Agua, and Barranca. A spur west into the Tusas Mountains served the lumber industry. One story behind the name of the Chili

Line has to do with the *ristras* hanging from roadside adobe homes along the route. Accounting for the spelling with an "i," which is the Anglo spelling for the dish of seasoned stew with meat, the conductors announced "chili stop" at cafes catering to riders. A famous literary capture of the little railroad's mystique was by Frank Waters in *The Woman at Otowi Crossing.* The heroine is modeled after Helen Chalmers who served riders in a small lunchroom on the route near Los Alamos.

In subsequent years, the Forest Service bought additional land for the Carson National Forest, and the village of Taos Junction south of Tres Piedras was largely abandoned in the 1930s. By 1941, the Chili Line was closed due to bankruptcy and the tracks dismantled. U.S. 285 follows the old railbed south and portions can be seen now just east of the highway, particularly around mile marker 369. All these "whistle stops" are gone except for Tres Piedras. The only surviving railroad structure there is the water tank which is a National Historic Site. It is next to the current Chili Line Depot Café, which survived as a dance hall, bar, and is now an excellent local eatery and town center across the highway from Mi Casita, qualifying it as a local palimpsest.

Humans in the Rocks Today

The most prominent rocks are popular with climbers following regulated access. This is consistent with the Forest Service's most recent Carson Land and Resource Management Plan Update, available at www.fs.usda.gov/goto/carsonforestplan. The Introduction states:

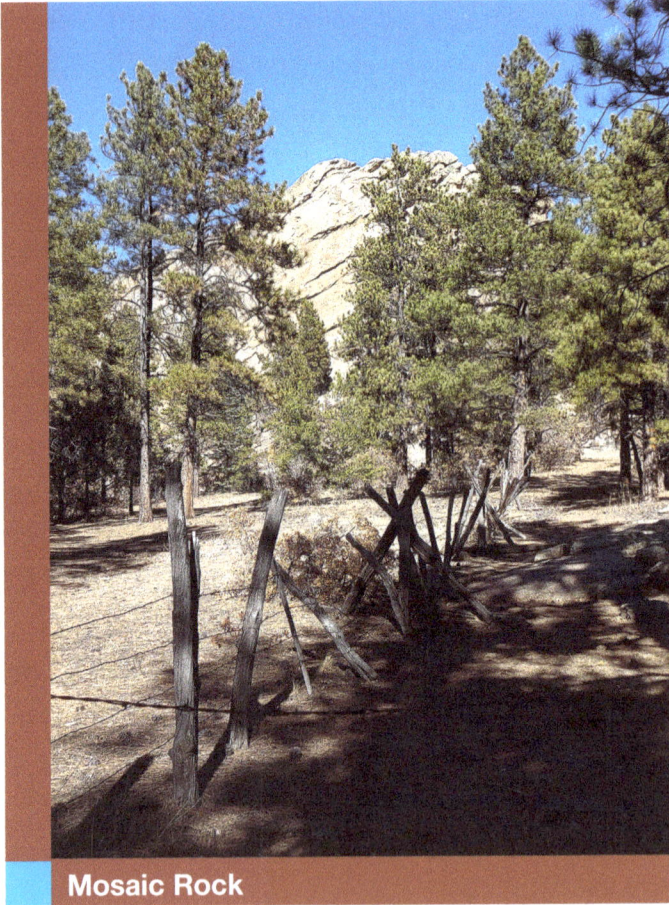

Mosaic Rock

By emphasizing multiple uses supported by healthy ecosystems
and working closely with our neighbors on shared interests, the
new Plan best meets the needs of the Carson National Forest
and its partners now and into the future.

The tallest rock is named Mosaic. Topping at 8,420 feet altitude, it is situated about a half mile west of Mi Casita. Approaching it on U.S. 64 and heading west from the
blinking light just past the Ranger Station, turn right onto
Forest Road 64J, pass a water tank and continue into the
Carson. This year I noticed the recent markings for wood

sale tree cutting and thinning to reduce fire risk among the ponderosas. While considering this, observe that ponderosa pine branches begin several feet up the trunk. This is a natural mechanism for resistance to low scrub fires. Another is the bark thickness.

The rutted road leads to a scattering of primitive campsites with a few tables and fireplace enclosures. Beware of the mud during monsoon and snow seasons. In about a half mile, the entrance to Mosaic Wall base is fenced with signage that advises caution when crossing adjacent private land. A Forest Service sign also tells us to avoid the rocks during peregrine falcon nesting season from March 1 to August 31. The trail is maintained by the New Mexico Resource and Advisory Group Access Fund. In researching the area, I was impressed to find organizations providing detailed descriptions of the rock-climbing site, including The Los Alamos Mountaineers, the Mountain Project, and Summit Posts. Clearly for the rugged young, some popular routes are named Dirty Diagonal, Chicken Heads, Mama Jugs, Serpent Face, and Techweenie. The dicey route Tres Piedras Crags sounds challenging; a successful summit climb reaches a cistern-like vernal pool. The panorama is far and wide.

Phenology, Architecture, and Biography at Mi Casita

Leopold Inspiration

The National Historic Registration that includes Mi Casita is titled "The Old Tres Piedras Administrative Site of the Carson National Forest." Before describing the built structures, let's continue exploring the human story. After Leopold moved from New Mexico to Wisconsin and eventually became the first Professor of Game Management at the University in Madison, he began restoring the now famous old farm and Shack family retreat. Biographer Curt Meine describes that in March, 1938, Aldo's journal recorded for the first time the spring "sky dance" of the woodcock. This experience initiated an important development in Leopold's environmental observations:

> From that point on, he began to pay much more attention to the sequence of events of the days and seasons. These detailed phenological notes began to fill up the pages of Leopold's journal (p. 382).

One anecdote records:

> On many a morning, Aldo went out to the garden in his bath-robe to quiet the cacophony [from daughter Estella's pet crow].... Leopold would put his insomnia to more satisfying use as he began to keep careful notes on the occurrence of various birdsongs (other than crows) as the basis for a phenologic study (p. 404).

Aldo wrote:

> Keeping records enhances the pleasure of the search and the chance of finding order and meaning in those events.

Phenology continues to be a major teaching commitment at the Aldo Leopold Foundation, founded by his children on the Shack land. The *Wisconsin Phenology Calendar* is published annually to share the family's legacy of keeping records and to encourage others to take up that habit. The 2021 edition states:

> Phenology is the study of the timing of seasonal events in nature. Wildlife emerging from hibernation, birds nesting and migrating, and flowers blooming are a few of the many phenologic events happening all around us, every year.... Those records alert us to when events are to be expected, and over time they help us understand how organisms are adapting to environmental shifts such as anthropogenic climate change (www.aldoleopold.org).

> The information includes awareness of time lags between events and detection, environmental variables including latitude, elevation, direction exposure, temperature, unique local climatic conditions, and the behavior of observers. Stan Temple, Professor Emeritus at the University of Wisconsin and Senior Fellow at the Aldo Leopold Foundation, explains that phenology is more than accounting, but rather for studying relationships of phenomena, from measurement for its own sake to dynamics of ecology, and for enjoyment and value. Out of this has come two significant scientific papers on climate change and phenology.

Phenology Now at Tres Piedras

No one has produced a thorough phenology study at our Mi Casita old historic site. I considered this challenge based on my weekly stewardship rounds for several years (with gaps during Covid-19 restriction periods). A worthy study should not dilute the quality of the science, so I decided to simply present the practice as a method to expand our knowledge and deepen our experience of this environment. Future opportunity awaits.

The Man-Made Historic Site

Robert G. Bailey, Ph.D., emeritus scientist at the U.S. Forest Service Rocky Mountain Research Station, described in *American Bungalow* magazine that Leopold chose a Craftsman-style bungalow design for the new supervisor's quarters in Tres Piedras:

> The simplicity would be consistent with his evolving philosophy of the land ethic, wilderness preservation, and the ecological benefits of small-housing living…. Advocates of Arts and Crafts philosophy of the time argued for harmony (rather than accumulation and opulence), natural design, and renewed contact with nature, all of which are embodied in the bungalow (p. 79).

Reproduction of an early pastel drawing of the cabin by Leopold hangs in the dining room.

Leopold's time here was brief. He came to the Carson in 1911 and had Mi Casita built in the summer of 1912 after moving the supervisor headquarters from Antonito, Colorado. His father sent furniture in the autumn. In April of 1913 he was caught in a winter storm when patrolling the Jicarilla District and suffered severe exposure. Acute kidney inflammation called Bright's Disease resulted. He

Aldo's Cabin Drawing

struggled back, and finally was hospitalized in Santa Fe. Estella had gone there pregnant, to be with her family.

Influence of the Place

This site was not an inert work location. Scholars and commentators have recognized the persuasive influence on Leopold's evolving thinking. Bailey summarizes:

> In the Carson he was faced with unhealthy land: overgrazed meadows, eroding gullies, and a lack of game. It was at this time that Leopold started to realize that the elements of the land—climate, vegetation, water, soil, geology, wildlife, and people—are integrated in a particular geographic area we now call an ecosystem.... Leopold argued that humans are part of ecosystems they inhabit; their actions should take into account the other elements of the systems.... Today we call this ecosys-

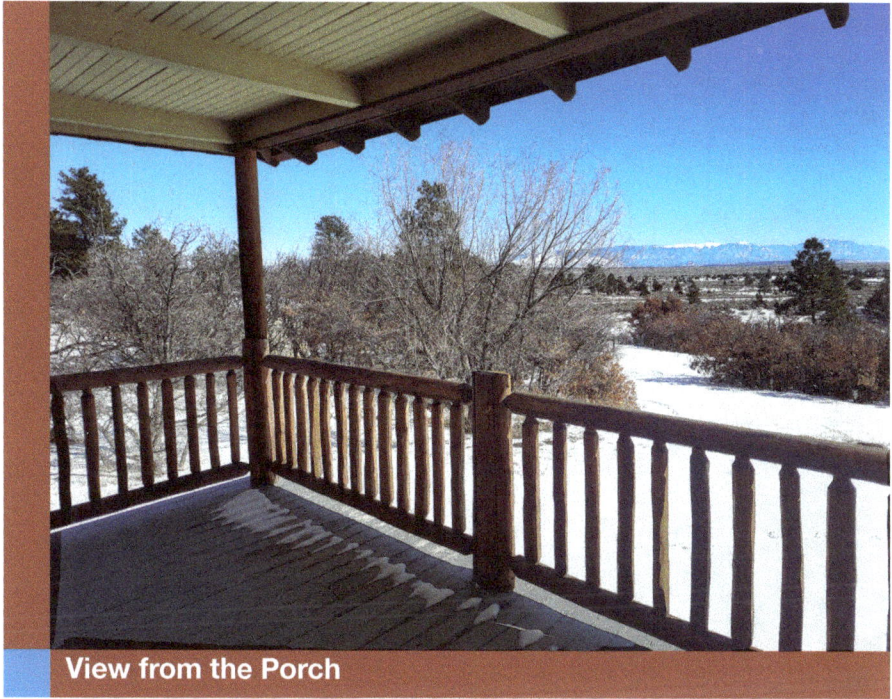

View from the Porch

tem management; Leopold later referred to it as the land ethic (p. 79–80).

A Stalwart Mi Casita and Carson Steward

Walter Perry joined the U.S. Forest Service in February of 1912 at age 38, having worked since teenage years as ranch hand, carpenter, and mining mechanic. He escaped from work in the Sierra Madre a day before the Mexican Revolution. As related in his 1938 memoir, edited and published by Les Joslin in 1999:

> Supervisor Hall pinned the Pine Tree badge on my shirt and told me to do honor to it. And that I tried to do for the next 25 years as forest guard, assistant forest ranger, forest ranger, scaler, lumberman, senior lumberman, and chief lumberman (p. 1).

Fireplace

Perry was assigned to the Carson in June, under Aldo Leopold's supervision. One of his first jobs was building the mammoth fireplace at Mi Casita of native *malpais* basaltic lava rock according to Leopold's specifications.

Before cowboy poetry became hip, Walt so expressed himself. One piece about an unpopular local sheep herder *patron,* written in December, 1912, ends:

> With apologies to Byron, and old Homer,
> "Father of Poets"—truly no misnomer,
> My muse I rein;
> Some ears this might not tickle,
> And eke I'd find myself in quite a pickle!

Editor Joslin comments that daughter Edith was particularly impressed by "The Big Brown Bungalow." She recalled the Leopold House being unoccupied during his sick leave. Acting Supervisor Raymond E. Marsh and his new bride Lillian were the next to live there, until the Forest Office was moved to its present location at Taos. An old photo shows Perry and family in front of the house about 1916, source not identified (p. 45).

The Perry family first lived in Tres Piedras for about five years in a refurbished miner's cabin. Edith wrote in her 1981 recollections of Mi Casita:

> Many happy hours were spent swinging from the big limb on the "hangman's tree" in the front yard. This had a history of usage as a place to hang fresh meat, and perhaps to skin out a deer carcass. The massive rocks were there to be climbed and I shrink from the memory of our daring climbs (p. 48).

Prior to Walt's appointment as Jicarilla District Ranger, the family homesteaded a small ranch south of town. His memoir tells us:

> I was some thirteen and a half years on the Carson Forest, and memory brings up many pleasant recollections, and not a few smiles connected with the men of that time.... As a matter of fact, on the Carson alone I wore out (more or less literally!) seven supervisors, and many changes in field personnel took place within that time (p. 121).

Perry maintained congenial contact afterward with Leopold. In a 1942 letter from Wisconsin, Aldo says:

> I appreciate your taking the trouble to write simply to acknowledge my few little publications,... I would hate to miss the chance to see you at the house and take you up to the farm. I have just finished my annual tree planting, and you are one of not very many people who would understand what the plantings are driving at (p. 181).

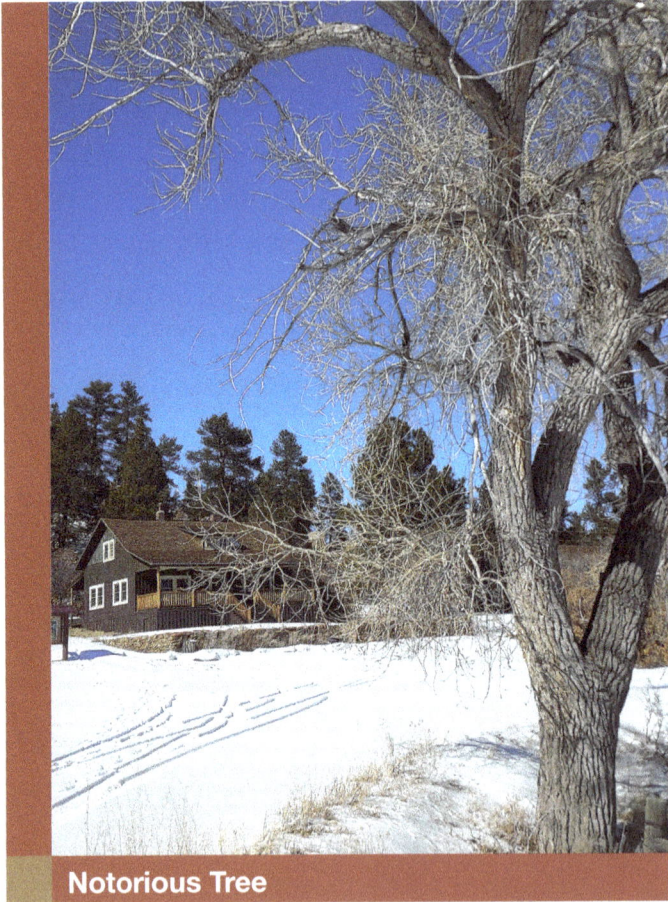

Notorious Tree

Joslin records in the memoir Epilogue that towards the end of his life, Walt wrote of his feelings for the forests in which he'd spent most of his working life in a letter to one of his daughters:

I know just how you feel, exactly how you feel, out under the pines. Many years I spent among them, looking at them, studying them, and listening to the whispering wind in their branches. They taught me much that was good for me and nothing to my hurt. They taught me patience and endurance, and tolerance for those who could not understand. I will probably walk very little or no more under the trees, but when you go there to refresh your soul, think of me as not being far away from you (p. 183).

You can meet Perry's great granddaughter, Sheila Roberts, chief cook at the Chili Line Depot Café, when she's not too busy making the best Reuben sandwich west of the Pecos. She donated the copy of Walt's memoir to the Mi Casita library.

4

From the Leopolds' Time to the Recent Restoration

National Historic Registration

The New Mexico Historic Preservation Division, part of the New Mexico Department of Cultural Affairs, describes the State and National Registers as:

> The fundamental building block of all preservation activity that:

- Recognizes important historic resources,
- Increases awareness of cultural heritage,
- Assists planning efforts,
- Opens doors to funding and tax credits. (nm.shpo@state. nm.us.)

The State Register is the official list of historic properties worthy of designation in New Mexico. The National Register is the official list of the nation's historic places worthy of preservation. It is administered by the National Park Service under the Secretary of the Interior.

Historic Plaque

The National Historic Registration document that in-cludes Mi Casita is titled "The Old Tres Piedras Adminis-trative Site of the Carson National Forest."

From the 1991 application prepared by Archaeologist Jon Nathan Young:

> The Old Tres Piedras Administrative Site is being nominated as a period piece—a perfectly preserved and classic representative of the early history of the National Forest Service.… The eight acres nominated include all of the buildings and structures his-torically associated with the site.… It belongs to a bygone era— when the administration of a National Forest essentially was a one-man operation. Then, that one man lived an isolated, in-tegrated existence.… The Old Tres Piedras Administrative Site Historic District stands as a constant reminder of the day when Aldo Leopold—founder of the American Wilderness Move-ment—administered Carson National Forest from its head-

quarters at Tres Piedras. More importantly, the Site is a living memorial to the very beginnings of the National Forest Service and the American conservation ethic.

The application continues:

Nestled in and around the eastern base of the central of the Tres Piedras [the three most prominent rocks arranged from east to west, standing 150 to 200 feet above the surrounding terrain], the Old Administrative Site is a collection of seven buildings and five other structures scattered over an eight-acre area. The buildings are: House, Root Cellar, Office, Barn, Shed,

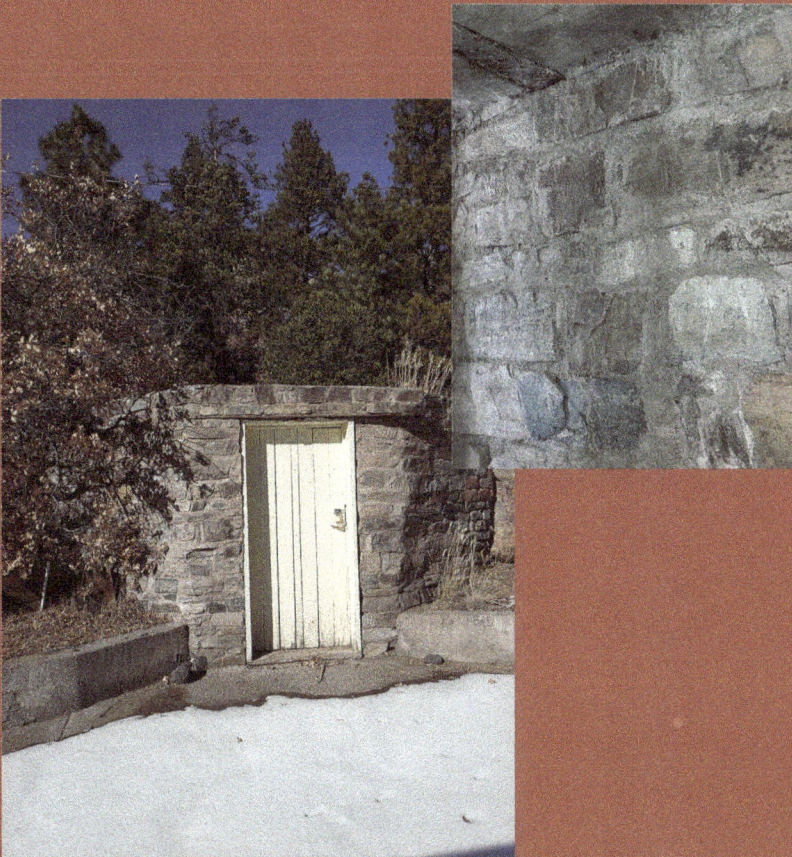

Root Cellar (above); Old Stone Cellar Wall (upper right)

Oil House, and Cistern. The structures are: Barn Corral, Pole Corral, Stock Tank, Vehicle Yard, and Water Impoundment.

Summaries from the 1991 detailed descriptions capture the essentials:

- Leopold built the House as his family residence. It has served continuously as a family residence from his day to ours.
- The Root Cellar was built at exactly the same time as the house, dug into loose granite gravel talus at the very base of the central Piedra. Except for a miniature basketball backboard tacked up above the entrance, the building and its appearance are substantially unaltered.
- The Office was built at the same time as the House, but at a spot six miles to the west. It was moved to its present location about fifty feet south of the House sometime soon after 1917.
- The Barn was built in 1931 and lies about a hundred feet north of the house. It was built originally as a shelter for livestock and their feed. Except for incidental storage, the Barn is not in use at the present time.

The 1931 barn burned in the 1950s and was replaced by the current building, still in active Forest Service use for utility storage.

- The Shed is not a contributing building to the historic designation. It was built in the 1980s to serve as a shelter for horses.
- The Oil House is not a contributing building. It was built in the late 1930s for the storage and dispensing of gas, oil, and kerosene. Rebuilt in 1951, it has been out of service for many years.
- The Cistern was constructed in the 1920s and is located about 275 feet south-southwest of the House. The 10-foot square shed protects the 25-foot-deep cistern, but it has not been in service for many years.
- The Barn Corral is part of the historic site, made of peeled ponderosa pine saplings and a portion formed by the vertical granite faces of the central Piedra. It was built as a pen for holding and feeding of livestock; it continues used for these purposes at the present time.

Old Ranger Office (top); Cistern Shed (bottom)

Current Wild Horse Adoption

- The Pole Corral is a historic structure, likely built in the late teens or early 1920s. Roughly circular with eight horizontal rows of peeled ponderosa saplings in each section, it was primarily a holding device for unbroken livestock. It continues as a gathering and holding area for the adoption program.
- The Stock Tank dates to the early or middle teens. It lies about 350 feet east of the house. Built to serve as a water source for livestock, it has not been so used for many years, but helps at present to control erosion.
- The Vehicle Yard is not historic, built in the middle 1980s and located about 225 feet southwest of the House. It is used for the semi-secure storage of vehicles and similar items.
- The Water Impoundment is historic and dates to the teens. It is fairly shallow, roughly circular in plan, and about 200 feet in diameter. Connected to the Cistern by a gravel infiltration gallery, it was built as a source of domestic water. It has not served this function for many, many years.

A clarification of the plaque is necessary. The precise wording should conform to the historic registration description. Our plaque has two variations. The first is its

Pole corral

use of Mi instead of Mia Casita, revealing that staff was not aware of the distinction when designing the plaque. The second is that the then supervising archaeologist and ranger directed that we attribute the Forest Service parent Agriculture Department, rather than the Interior Department that administers the historic registration program.

Mi Casita After the Leopolds
After the Leopold years, Mi Casita was a staff residence and utility building for the Forest Service. National events such as World War I, the Great Depression, and World War II had severe impacts. I found gaps in the documented history of the cabin. Bailey reports significant modifications by the year 2000, including raising the roof pitch to provide more second floor room for the Civilian Conservation Corps workers in the 1930s. Original wood frame windows were replaced with aluminum. The exterior was painted off-white. The beamed ceilings were covered with foam tiles. The pine trim and fireplace were painted.

Colors, finishes, and doors had been changed or replaced to suit subsequent occupants' tastes. Fortunately, the Forest Service had kept the house's original footprint in keeping with the Arts and Crafts aesthetic (p. 88).

After eighteen months of recuperation, most at his family home in Burlington, Iowa, Leopold resumed Forest Service desk job duties. He began in the Albuquerque Office of Grazing, then became coordinator of the district's new Game and Fish Program. This assignment took him around New Mexico and Arizona drumming up support for game conservation "to promote the protection and enjoyment of wild things" as he wrote in the Christmas 1915 *Pine Cone,* Official Bulletin of the New Mexico Game Protective Association. During World War I, his work shifted to Secretary of the Albuquerque Chamber of Commerce, but he continued naturalist studies and conservation initiatives. As the Forest Service returned to peacetime plans, he accepted the job as Assistant Forester in charge of operations, the second highest position in a district that spanned twenty million acres in Arizona and New Mexico. According to Julianne Lutz Warren in *Aldo Leopold's Odyssey,*

> What drew Leopold's particular attention, though, were the larger issues of land-use patterns and their consequences.... No job could have better positioned Assistant District Forester Leopold to think seriously about human-used landscapes in their entirety (p. 52).

The grazing permit system he organized improved rangeland health by limiting the cattle allotments allowed each permit holder in exchange for their exclusive use of a land section. In his operations role, Leopold also began developing wilderness designation for the Gila area which was subsequently instituted, the first in the nation. The growing family's home in Albuquerque at 135 Fourteenth Street SW is still a residence, part of the registered Aldo Leopold Neighborhood Historic District. His years in New Mexico ended in 1924 on appointment to the Service's Forest Products Laboratory in Madison, Wisconsin.

Life in the Gap

I found an engaging window into Forest Service life in the 1930s through *The Lookout Cookbook, a 1938 USFS Manual with 1939 Supplement*:

> Introduction: The idea back of this book is to furnish tried and approved recipes in amounts suitable for one or two men which can be prepared from the food furnished the lookouts. The persons who furnished recipes were requested to refrain from calling for any food supplies not furnished. The book was tried out by nearly a hundred lookouts, smokechasers, small crews, etc., during the 1937 season and their comments and suggestions are included.

Chapter headings include Household Suggestions, Food Facts, Breads, Sandwich Suggestions, Soups, Ways of Preparing Meat Varieties, Sauces, Entrees, Vegetables, Egg Dishes, Salads, Cookies, Cakes, Desserts, Puddings, Beverages, Pastry. Some distinctive recipe names are Mulligan, Salmon Wiggle, and Pep Cocktail. It ends with

> A Guide for Meal Planning describing 1) Growth and Protective Foods which Help Prevent Nervous Disorders, Scurvy, Rickets, and Infections; 2) Body Building and Regulating Foods for Muscle, Bone, and Teeth; and 3) Energy Giving Foods.

The Bungalow Restoration

With funding available to honor the Forest Service Centennial, plans were initiated in 2005 to renovate the house exterior and interior as closely as possible to the configuration it held when designed in 1911 and built in 1912 under the direction of Leopold. A detailed restoration plan was developed by Recreation Solutions, a USDA Forest Service Enterprise Unit. This program provides technical support services, including historical management, restoration, and engineering. Department of Interior Standards were followed for the combined "Historic Restoration and Rehabilitation as Treatments." The plan stated:

> A restoration date of 1911 has been selected, and the appearance, form, and feel of the house will reflect that date. As is the case with most restoration projects, some compromises must be made for the sake of utility. Since the Forest Service will offer the house to the public as a place of reflection and scholarly pursuits, it must comply with safety codes.

After Carson Archaeologist William Westbury and Supervisor Kendall Clark approval, Tres Piedras Ranger Ben Romero is credited with implementation. Robert G. Bailey, scientist at the Fort Collins Rocky Mountain Research Station, summarized the Leopold history and process in *American Bungalow Magazine,* Fall 2014, edition:

> Windows were replaced, the electrical wiring and plumbing were redone, and decades of paint were scraped away. Today the interior glows with the patina of old wood and period colors (p. 88).

Copies of this article and the 22-page Restoration Plan are now collected in the Mi Casita Library for staff, visiting students, and scholars. Multiple professional contractors and volunteers engaged in this work, particularly the HistoriCorps Program. There is a YouTube video of Ben leading a post-restoration tour. Books were donated to the cabin library in his honor.

Restored Living Room

Note that this 2005–6 restoration was not for a static museum display. With aspirations to be "a place of reflection and scholarly pursuits," compromises were recognized for the sake of utility and safety. Electric wiring was updated; smoke alarms, new kitchen appliances, gas furnace, and water heater were installed. We face those issues now with ongoing restoration and maintenance efforts, possibly even more so. During the past few years, we advised visitors about wildlife in the rocks such as rattlesnakes, hanta virus from mouse urine in the cellar, and rusty nails. New carpentry includes interior stair safety features and handicap access. Fire danger is greater now due to our long drought, so in the recent chimney repair planning, Ranger Angie decided not to allow use of the historic fireplace in the foreseeable future. Second floor bedroom windows are 18 feet above the ground, but the historic small size does not meet modern exit code for an escape ladder. Last, as I edit this in May of 2022, the Forest Service is considering closure of the Carson to the public as the largest wildfire in New Mexico history rages to the southeast in the Santa Fe National Forest.

5

Renewal Initiatives

Creation of the Leopold Writing Program

On completion of the restoration, advocates' attention turned to programming for Mi Casita. Albuquerque architect Anthony Anella had authored *Saving the Ranch: Conservation Easement Design in the American West.* In 2011, he was serving on the Board of the Wisconsin Aldo Leopold Foundation and engaged an influential group in brainstorming possibilities for Mi Casita. That group included the Carson Supervisor, Leopold Foundation Executive Director, Carson Public Affairs Officer, Tres Piedras District Ranger, and Cofounder of the Rocky Mountain Land Library. The Spring Creek Project in Oregon was considered as a possible model.

Organized as an independent nonprofit in 2012, the Leopold Writing Program expresses the mission "to inspire an ethic of caring for our planet by cultivating diverse voices through the spoken and written word." It is structured with three components, as described now on the website www.leopoldwritingprogram.org:

1) An essay contest for 6–12th grade students throughout New Mexico, "giving voice to young writers most vulnerable to the consequences of environmental inaction,"

2) A lecture series "featuring a distinguished environmental thinker to highlight challenging and urgent conservation needs," and

3) One-month residency experiences for two emerging and midcareer environmental writers per year at Mi Casita "interested in reshaping the cultural story of humans relating to Nature."

On Becoming Steward

Since the program's initiation in 2012 through 2021, there have been twenty-one residents. They are identified and described on the website. I will share my own meaningful experiences with this group, but first spin the yarn about how my role at Mi Casita and relationship with the writing residents developed. When retiring to full time "being here now" in our Taos vacation house, Annette and I sought community service participation. Despite fifty-plus years being intermittent visitors and semi-local in Albuquerque, there is much more to know about Taos as full-timers. That includes how people regard you. Once in a conversation with a Norteño old guy, fielding the usual questions about where are you from, he asked me, "But where do you vote?" I learned another definition of being a local.

Botanic Diversification

Recapturing organic gardening and naturalist exposures from childhood, I joined the Taos chapter, Native Plant Society of New Mexico. The president Claudia spotted me as useful, saying "You have time, tools, and truck." She accurately nailed me because I had long adopted the personal motto from the Masons:

> Towards a widening sphere of usefulness.

This derives from the old New Jersey school I attended. Newark Academy was founded in 1774 by the Presbyterian colonists to train people (women included) for service in the new civic and government agencies. But the British burned the school in the War of 1812, and the Presbyterians could not afford to rebuild. The Masons, including some of our Founding Fathers, restored the building. That's why George Washington signed the cornerstone, still preserved, and the school's new motto expressed Masonic usefulness.

After initiation in helping rebuild the wind-blown Native Plant Society greenhouse at the Gutierrez Agriculture Center, I was elected to the Taos chapter board. The board needed help arranging field trips, in particular finding guides. Having explored national forests camping and fly fishing here, I made calls around the local U.S. Forest Service. I was referred to Bonnie Woods, restoration specialist stationed in Tres Piedras. Yes, that is her real name as Forest Service staff, given by her carpenter father growing up in Arizona.

Bonnie led Native Plant Society outings to the Valle Vidal, including a visit to New Mexico's preserve of bristlecone pines. As they go, these are just adolescents, only about a thousand years old. Another trip went to the Stewart Meadows Preserve about fifteen miles north of Tres Piedras, an early twentieth century homestead along the Rio San Antonio coming off San Antonio Peak. Then in the spring of 2015, Bonnie called me asking for volunteer help. One of the 2014 writing residents was Bonnie Harper-Lore, an accomplished botanist from Minnesota. With extensive experience helping public organizations like state highway departments develop native plant installations, she proposed planting a native garden at Mi Casita to the Tres Piedras ranger.

Recent photos of Mi Casita show a four-foot high stone retaining wall for the front earthen area that extends about fifty feet in front of the cabin. Very early photos, indicated by absence of cabin stair railings, show a slope instead. I cannot verify when the wall was built but will guesstimate it was an early 1930s Civilian Conservation Corps project. In 2015, a stretch of bare soil extended along the sixty feet width and three feet depth from the wall to a stone pathway. As an Historic Site, the district archaeologist needed to study the proposed garden area for artifacts given that we planned to dig. He did several inspection holes, and the only find was a rusty 1950s toy car. The cabin had housed a succession of Forest Service staff families. Another childhood artifact of unknown age is a weathered old swing, attached by ropes to the limb of a large ponderosa on the cabin's north side, about fifteen feet up.

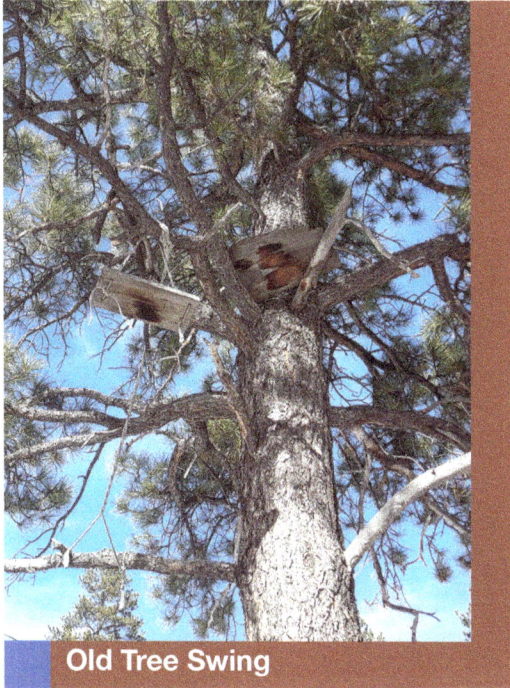

Old Tree Swing

Bonnie H-L developed an extensive list of recommend-
ed plants, worthy of a demonstration project. We started
with the thirty feet length on the north side of the steps
in the wall's middle. Besides invasive cheatgrass, the only
growth there was a native thicket creeper along part of
the wall top. Bonnie W and I went shopping locally and
obtained a few Rocky Mountain penstemon forbs and
Apache plume and Woods rose shrubs. Bonnie H-L joined
us for the initial digging in. I transplanted some gaillardia
blanket flowers, prairie coneflower, and orange globe mal-
low from home and spread a seed mix. The mulch was my
favorite organic, attractive New Mexico pecan shell. Then
water, water, water to foster establishment. A contingent

Mi Casita Garden Now

from the Taos Native Plant Society chapter installed some identification signs that were surplus from an educational garden project at Millicent Rogers Museum. I was blessed soon to receive a copy of *A Sand County Almanac* inscribed:

> Richard, I just wanted to thank you for your hard work on July 24th. We all did more than any one person should have. So, I wanted to be sure you have your very own copy of the book that took me to Tres Piedras! Thank you for your continued involvement. Sincerely, Bonnie Harper-Lore.

As Nature influenced our propagation, I decided to follow her direction. The forbs struggled with summer drought and winter cold. No seeds sprouted. The native shrubs established themselves well. Bonnie Woods moved on to New Hampshire, but the presence of a garden became pleasing to me, staff, and visitors such as the writer residents. Therefore, I decided to extend planting along the south wall with several hardy Apache plumes and added specimens of native mountain mahogany and millefolium fernbush. Five years later, they all have survived, even flourished, and add to the ecological vitality. I admit that this garden is not a verified historic restoration, as we have no evidence of such in Leopold days, or later. But it is a contribution of valid diversification in the cabin botanic environment. And as nothing is completely entitled to us humans, pocket gophers still assert their territorial imperative, but have settled into peaceful coexistence with the garden.

6

Resident, Steward, and Visitor Discoveries

Walkabouts and *Paseandos*

When the concept "walkabout" came to me as a way of describing these stories, I had to check my cultural correctness. The online Oxford Dictionary confirmed my intent, defining "a journey on foot undertaken by an Australian Aboriginal in order to live in the traditional manner." If we allow hiking boots and respectful practice by others, several Leopold Writing Program residents have left contributions from their walkabouts. The esteemed Taos author Frank Waters described the practice of *paseando* ("strolling") on his land under El Salto Peak. With some imagination, this can be seen in the distance directly east from the porch of Mi Casita across the Rio Grande Gorge and Taos Plateau. Waters expresses the idea, more than the literal meaning of the word, in *Mountain Dialogues*:

> I have been more susceptible to the silent exhortations of the
> spirits of the living land. Our communion with these nonverbal

spirits is achieved in that strange element of silence in which our inner selves are as much at home as our outer selves in the world of multitudinous sound. For in it, the human spirit discovers its own identity and its kinship with the spirits of distant stars (p. 55).

During one of my regular visits for cabin stewardship and librarian duties, 2021 Leopold Writing Program resident Eve Bratman showed me a unique artifact with a feeling of amazement. As she later wrote in the Writing Program newsletter, *El Piñón:*

Coming down from the rocks another bright Saturday morning, I found something profound. Tucked well under the shelter of a rocky ledge was a weather-worn, slightly tattered Catholic mass prayerbook and a colorful chunk wooden rosary.... I sat back down and flipped to the passage that was bookmarked by a frail green cloth page marker.

The page offered the gospel of Luke 21, 25:33: "There will be signs in the sun and moon and stars, and upon the earth distress of nations bewildered by the roaring of sea and waves: men fainting for fear and for expectation of the things that are coming on the world; for the powers of heaven will be shaken.

I will stop the quotation there, but recommend you read the essay in full on the www.leopoldwritingprogram.org website for Eve's thoughtful application of this verse to our time. The missal and rosary are now on the artifact shelf in the cabin.

Another contribution was left on the cabin desk by 2016 resident Andrew Gulliford. He and colleague Dr. Dugald Owen from Ft. Lewis College compiled a bird list "from two days wandering on the property."

Pine Siskin, Spotted Towhee, Mourning Dove, Pygmy Nuthatch, Western Bluebird, Brewer's Sparrow, Northern Flicker, Hairy Woodpecker, Say's Phoebe, Mountain Chickadee,

Gray or Dusky Flycatcher, House Wren, American Robin, Plumbeous Vireo, Great Horned Owl, Common Raven, Broad-tailed Hummingbird, Violet-green Swallow, Western Wood-Pe-wee, White-breasted Nuthatch, Brown-headed Cowbird, Williamson's Sapsucker, Dark-eyed junco, Chipping Sparrow, Hammond Flycatcher, Lesser Goldfinch, Blue-gray Gnatcatcher, Townsend's Solitaire, Hermit Thrush.

Laura Pritchett in May 2018 penciled additions:

Downy Woodpecker, Steller's Jay, Turkey vulture, Red-tailed Hawk, Yellow Warbler, Rufous-sided Towhee, Western Tanager, Evening Grosbeak.

These erudite lists, phenology of sorts, were left casually. I confess to needing my Audubon Guide to record the names properly here. In June 2019, resident Laura Paskus added her observation of forty-four birds in the Guest Register, listed later. Finally on this avian topic, 2020 resident Priyanka Kumar wrote an expressive article, "Where Birds Whispered in My Ear," available in *El Piñón*, Fall 2020.

A Steward Discovery

Sometime in my medical career, I became fond of quoting Louis Pasteur who said in an 1854 lecture, "In the fields of observation, chance favors only the prepared mind." Sometimes I've abbreviated the phrase, omitting the *only*. I invoke it now for our theme of fostering attentiveness to both the communal man-made and more-than-human world. Here's a small story from one of my Mi Casita walkabouts. My canine sidekick Troi wears a bear bell on an orange kerchief when exploring the cabin environs to cue my monitoring her. We model the traditions of both Pasteur and Leopold. In the July essay of *A Sand County Almanac,* Aldo wrote:

Barn Water Tank Site

> We sally forth, the dog and I, at random. He has paid scant re-
> spect to all these vocal goings-on [morning bird songs], for to
> him the evidence of tenantry is not song, but scent. Any illiter-
> ate bundle of feathers, he says, can make a noise in a tree. Now
> he is going to translate for me the olfactory poems that who-
> knows-what silent creatures have written in the summer night
> (p. 46).

Maybe being more of a wordsmith than musician, this
practice appeals to me greatly. So, I follow Troi as she pursues a trail. About two years ago, she led me behind the
cabin, uphill into the rocks. Instead of a creature poem, we
found a Mi Casita relic. I came upon a concrete slab about
twenty-five by thirty feet. Asking around, it was novel to
Forest Service staff. Maybe an old echo from Edward Ab-
bey had me surmising it was formerly a fire lookout base.

Positioned above the barn roof, the view stretched east across the valley.

Troi led me there again last month. Actively collecting material for this book, I again raised the origin question with new staff. They had no information about old fire lookouts, but Officer Ricardo Leon said a pad for a water tank made sense. Following that clue, I went back to the details on the 1991 Historic Registration application and found no mention of such. The next historic source I consulted was Robert G. Bailey's 2014 *American Bungalow* magazine article about the cabin restoration. In describing the interior, he said,

> The house boasted a bathroom with a tub and a kitchen sink some 30 years before its water supply was established in a tank atop a granite outcrop behind the house.

However, on another exploration to the south about twenty-five yards, positioned above the rear cabin porch, I found a cement cube with another adjacent slab. A pipe protruded, and twenty feet below, an old bent bar appeared to be a valve handle. The eight-foot square cube had a top opening, as if it were meant to collect ice and run off water. Much as I'd enjoy verifying it was the base of a fire lookout tower, I now conclude this was the house water source, and the north platform was a tank for the barn.

Wild Discoveries

Natural dynamics create developments in the Mi Casita biosphere. A previously overlooked small tree behind the cabin bloomed distinctively four springs ago. On closer look, I identified an apricot, *Prunus armeniaca*. They have

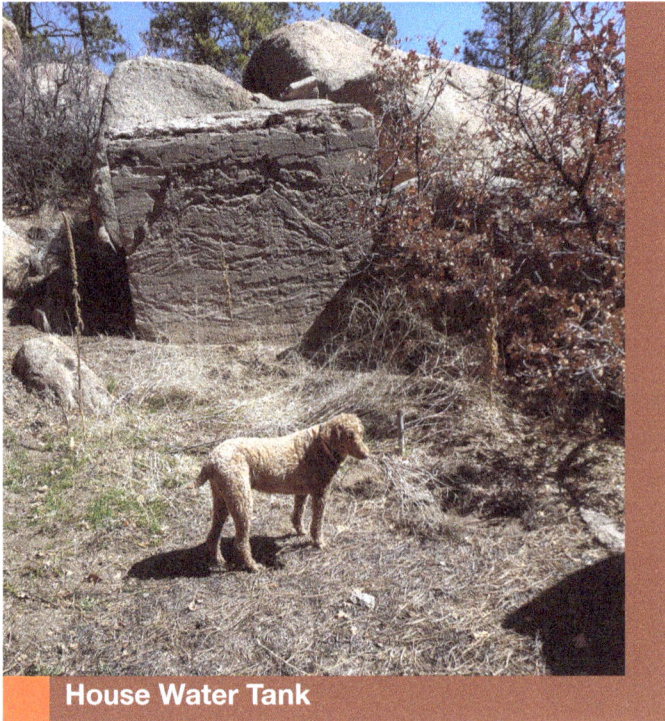

House Water Tank

been in the Taos Valley since seventeenth-century settlement, brought by the Franciscans. Originally from Chi-
na, apricots were distributed across the Middle East to
Europe. The small trees are vigorously feral here, but the
fruiting is notoriously erratic in our mountain climate. By
feral, I distinguish them from native plants, but now growing wild since the original domestic planting. The common old fruit are small; larger varieties were brought from
California after nineteenth-century railroad access.

Intrigued, I searched the environs more carefully and discovered another apricot tree. They both flank the historic
root cellar behind the cabin, suggesting deliberate placement where water flows down from the rocks. To restore
them from years of neglect, I pruned dead wood and re-

moved sun-blocking Gambel oaks. The few blooms did not fruit that year, likely vulnerable to drought and frost effects. When winter dormant, I pruned for open center productivity. Curious about their age with trunks several inches thick, I engaged Forester Robin to do coring research. Her procedure yielded an age of eighty-five years. This would be after the Leopolds' time, likely planted by a later resident Ranger. We were rewarded with some fruit that spring. Never one to underestimate natural vigor, 2020 resident Emily found a new specimen several yards away, likely enabled by a feeding bird or rodent spreading seeds. In 2022, the south tree I rehabbed was showing dozens of blossoms, but they were blown off by more fierce than usual May winds, maybe a climate change effect.

Another wild find happened when carpenter friend Louis was working on replacing the warped cabin stairs. He noticed an unusual viny plant just under the southeast roof corner. Unfamiliar to me, he said, "That looks like hops." Hmm, checking my native plant guidebook, I discovered that there is a native hops variety here. However, my Native Plant Society consultant botany professor John Ubelaker said that the native species is very rare. Friend Greg who raises a crop took a look, and said "Yup, definitely a common, commercial hops." Telling this story to Sheila at the Chili Line Depot Café, the great granddaughter of Walter Perry, she said, sure, the German settlers commonly grew hops to brew their own beer. I decided a bird was enjoying the flower cones from an old garden while perched on the roof edge, and the seeds found a fertile home to be wild, reproducing on their own. I add some community nurture with water during dry spells and it is flourishing in a third season.

Artifacts Inside

As we make a lower floor circuit of the house indoors, the walls and mantle show seven photos of Aldo and Estella, apparently framed at the restoration. They are all familiar, even iconic, to readers of the Leopold story tomes, many listed in our library overview. I have learned that the University of Wisconsin maintains an extensive Aldo Leopold Archive. Being digitalized, thousands of photos are recorded and available to authors and scholars. The story goes that Aldo brought back a Leica camera from a forestry inspection trip to Germany in 1934, and oldest son Starker became a prolific family photographer. In addition, many early photos from around Tres Piedras are under Forest Service copyright, likely the source on cabin refurnishing for the restoration.

The stairs leading to the second floor have racks of shelves on both the right and left sides. The right side faces the living room and now contains the cabin library. The left side shelves are shallow and display six pieces of heavy glazed dinnerware with Forest Service logos. Their journey to the cabin began with an offer by a retired staff member to the Questa Ranger District a few years ago. Officer Eric Garner, stationed there at the time, inquired if I could display them at the cabin. Some stain and front quarter round molding allowed me to make the shelves secure for what you can see now. Research identified them of 1930s vintage.

Looking carefully at the photo's upper left, you can see the missal and rosary found by Eve Bratman. Several other objects are also displayed there, following the rule that

Indoor Artifacts

if rusted, it is not garbage, but someone's potential data. And the top shelf ponderosa pinecones have distinction as "fractals from the forest."

The Guest Register

Somehow in 2016, a small journal book inscribed *Mi Casita Guest Register, Tres Piedras District, Carson National Forest* appeared on the large dining room desk. At first, I thought it was donated by then Ranger Chris Furr or his wife Kathryn who provided cabin care services, particularly for the Leopold Writing Program residents. Now Ranger in the Methow Valley District of the Okanogan-Wenatchee National Forest, I recently asked him. But he said no, they were not the donors.

The first entry in the Guest Register on August 13, 2016, covers two pages by resident Andy Gulliford from Durango, Colorado. The similarity between the hand-printed inscription and his entry suggests he was the book's donor. A few excerpts:

> To see the rain cover the Sangre de Cristos from Leopold's porch was stunning. I don't think the view has changed much

in the century since he built his house, except for the cell phone tower masquerading as a ponderosa pine tree.…

I think his presence is here in this house and certainly on the porch if you sit in that Leopold bench.…

It was great in my time at the bungalow to have Dr. Stanley Temple from the University of Wisconsin-Madison come to see the house.… I had my own tutorial by a senior Leopold Fellow at the Leopold Foundation.

The Leopold Bench Story

Andy's reference to the Leopold Bench requires an explanation. No evidence confirms their existence before Leopold built several for the family's outdoor living at the now famous Shack in Wisconsin. However, the distinctive and practical design he created has become totemic. The Wisconsin Leopold Foundation held workshops on building the benches, and I obtained plans from their education staff. Two now grace my home fire circle. Getting back to Andy Gulliford's reference, a bench now sits on the front porch at Mi Casita. I was told that a local Tres Piedras wood mill made it for the 2007 restoration. Yes, now a totem.

Wildfire Crews, A Rugged Winter Resident, and Visiting Students

Perceiving Andy's wise metamessage, I began encouraging visitors and writer residents to use the book. Maybe we can call this stewardship of the Mi Casita legacy. I reproduce the entries as written now. The next came from Tres Piedras District and Carson National Forest stalwarts. On October 21, 2016, Luke Jourdet wrote for the "AZCC Vet Crew" (Arizona Conservation Corps):

A Leopold Bench

We have been doing wildfire effects monitoring; as far as the terrain goes, this is the most challenging yet.... The rocks in the back are awesome. They remind me of the Black Hills, South Dakota.

Maya Kapoor, in transition from journalism in Tucson to the *High Country News* in Colorado, said on December 27:

Being in the Leopold House during winter had its challenges—mainly power and heat going out when it got windy—but I loved hiking in the snow to the rock formations and looking for tracks.

Working the Hondito Fire, Michael Reichling from Pine, Arizona, recorded on May 22, 2017:

Making friends and working to provide information to the community.

On May 23, Tom Kuzmic, forester, wrote, and eight students/teachers signed:

> Oklahoma State University was here, to celebrate the spirit and inspiration of Aldo and to "Think like a mountain."

Samantha Rosado, environmental scientist, added this Leopold quote:

> Girdling the old oak to squeeze the last crop out of the backyard has the same finality as burning the furniture to keep warm.

A Writing Program Board Service

One day while I was tending the new garden, the Writing Program Board was meeting at the cabin. Founder Tony Anella saw I could be useful, particularly since none of the members lived in Taos County. During my subsequent two years of board tenure helping with administrative matters such as website refinement and applicant recruitment, I continued the hands-on cabin stewardship. One result was that board members offered to help with maintenance such as repainting the porch floor and oiling the rail. In recognition, I left a note in the Guest Register honoring their participation.

> A special Memorial Day for the traditions we value, May 28–29, 2017.

A Music and Poetry Creative Residency

In the 2017 applications for a residency, two friends submitted a proposal for an original chamber music and poetry piece based on Leopold's transformative experience killing a wolf and watching the fierce green fire fade from her eyes. "Transformed by Fire" was performed to full audiences twice in Taos, accompanied by the Taos Community Chorus. Both artists, composer pianist Andrea Clearfield from Philadelphia and poet Ariana Kramer from Taos, left gracious messages of gratitude in the Guest Register.

Traveling Forest Service and Community Contributions

U.S. Forest Service staff are a mobile lot, and Ranger Chris Furr went shooting the route to Washington state. During the ensuing year, I held the fort while acting rangers interested in the job came quarterly. Lydia La Belle de Rios, experienced in Vermont and Colorado, said,

> Inspiring place to ponder the privilege of caring for the land and serving the people.

Lydia's husband Gregorio, originally from Neembucu, Paraguay, added,

> Beautiful place!! Thank you for the opportunity to visit here! Great history!!

On September 15, 2017, a group from the Native Plant Society of New Mexico visited, including members from Las Cruces, Aztec, Placitas, Sandia Park, Ranchos de Taos, and Taos, plus El Paso and Graham, Texas. Cheryl from El Paso wrote:

> Several years ago, I came to this Aldo Leopold house and saw the terrible condition it was in, including the pink fireplace. We were told at the time it would improve some day when funds were available. I am so glad I came back today and have seen the amazing transformation of this historical site. Thank you so much for your efforts in restoring this special icon of conservation.

Emelie and Glenn from Taos added,

> We were delighted to finally get to see the interior of the Leopold house and to see the restoration efforts. We eagerly look forward to the program to allow admirers like us to rent it for a few nights—we hope. Aldo is one of my heroes.

Of Beavers and Rangeland Ecology

Ben Goldfarb shares with Leopold a Yale degree, now called a Master of Environmental Management from the School of Forestry and Environmental Studies. He completed *Eager, The Surprising Secret Life of Beavers and Why They Matter* during his 2017 writing residency. Having explored widely during his research and field experience, he invited rangeland ecologist Matt Barnes and his partner Emily to visit. They were also traveling the West, from his work on Montana ranches to exploring future sites in Colorado. They both left Guest Register entries in September. Matt described the extensive influence he felt from Leopold's writings. Emily expressed hope "we can take a small dose of greatness from these walls as we continue our travels."

Then the Register has a lovely entry from Elise Rose, Ben's wife who came for a brief visit. I learned she was completing a nurse midwife program back at Yale and said beneath her drawing of mountain peaks:

> I came to stay with my own Aldo, and this place is so beautiful. We wandered the forest and went searching for Great Horned Owls and listened for coyotes at night. Thank you for opening this space up for Ben to write—it has enriched his book, I'm sure.

Ben and I connected easily as northeastern kids with naturalist interests, and we valued our experiences with Am-

Bean Pickers

herst College, Ben as undergraduate and me as a parent around my son Dan's time there. During the week when Elise visited, they came to our home for a harvest gathering and enjoyed picking red beans and blue corn. My decades of encountering beaver dams on the Rio Hondo along the Taos Ski Valley access road made interesting story swapping. Here are gleanings from Ben's two-page Register letter:

Just as Aldo taught the world to love and appreciate wolves for their vital ecological function, so too am I singing the praises of a maligned and misunderstood species. Not that my pedestrian prose will ever attain his heights, but the animating idea—that the destruction of keystone species leads to the unraveling of landscapes, and that ecological salvation lies in restoration—dovetails closely with "thinking like a mountain." …Although Richard is no fan of the mice (and I probably wouldn't be either, if I ran this place), I enjoyed hearing them scamper around; their rustling made me feel less alone... For the land, Ben.

Inspiration for Students

On March 21, 2018, twelve students from the Class of 2019 Master of Environmental Management program at Western State Colorado University recorded:

> We enjoyed an insightful and invigorating discussion this night during our 6 day tour of Northern New Mexico. We were all thrilled by this opportunity. Thank you, Forest Service!

Clarinda Wilson, UW Class of 2008, added:

> As a graduate of the wildlife ecology degree at the University of Wisconsin-Madison, it was a dream spending the night in an area that was so influential to the founder of my program.

On April 15, 2019, Gabriela Zaldumbide wrote:

> Dear Reader, Today I arrived at the Leopold House with fellow Master of Environmental Management students from Western Colorado University. Upon seeing the cabin, my heart held a sense of fulfillment. I completed my undergraduate studies at the University of Wisconsin-Madison where I majored in Wildlife Ecology, the same department Leopold started upon his arrival in Wisconsin,... I'll reflect upon Leopold's contributions to modern ecology and contemplate how I can improve upon them myself.

Another piece unsigned on April 17 beneath a bold "Thanks from Western Colorado University":

> The Master in Environmental Management program has returned! We have been inspired as land managers to make waves in our public lands agencies. During our trip across Northern New Mexico, a group of us gained insight for developing a DIGITAL JUNIOR RANGER Program for our National Historic Trails. Stay tuned!

And a final WCU inspired contribution, also unsigned:

Howdy, The moment our group arrived, I felt a sense of peace.... I am studying forest and ecosystem ecology under the Integrative Public Land Management track.... I will travel the globe to research pre and post wildfire disturbances to our ecosystem.... I hope you continue doing great work and always remember ALDO LEOPOLD!!

In May, we hear expressions of gratitude from Oklahoma State University students Tom K., Byron Murray, and Carmen Hardin.

On July 27, a long message from the "SWAP" Crew is individually signed by twenty-six people. The leader describes:

Hallowed Ground—I had made arrangements to stay in the Leopold cabin for a number of months. The plan was to bring a large crew of wildlife students from two vastly different eco-regions—New Mexico and Tennessee. The "SWAP" program provides once-in-a-lifetime opportunities to students from underserved communities.... These are the students who will one day protect these wild and majestic lands—somehow I think Aldo would approve of his young and boisterous house guests.

Continuing Naturalist and Writer Commentary

In June 2018, the Native Plant Society of New Mexico, Taos chapter, brought in retired U.S. Forest Service botanist and biologist Renee Galeano-Popp from Colorado. After a seminar on native conifers and pine cones at my home, she visited Mi Casita with me and recorded:

Thank you, Aldo Leopold for all of your books, teachings, and legacy. As a former Biologist on the North Kaibab Ranger District, I have still never quite forgiven you and Teddy Roosevelt for your years of advocating predator control/removal there. I'm glad you later changed your mind and again thank you for your legacy with the USFS and beyond.

Engaged by the visit with his friend Ben Goldfarb the previous year, Matt Barnes applied and was chosen for a June

2018 Writing residency. I got to know him during several stewardship visits, and he would agree on having a different identity than writer. In the Guest Register, Matt describes a quixotic course in academics, but found direction in wildlife and natural resource endeavors. He wrote:

> Leopold inspired me to work with large carnivores. I also became a rangeland scientist. Years later, with Leopold in mind, I was finally able to integrate these two things: livestock grazing management and coexistence with potential predators.

His entry proceeds to extensive details of work in Montana and Wyoming, now realizing that Aldo was a founder of range management. In his Harwood Museum talk, Matt articulated how this came from Leopold's thinking ahead of his time in ecology applied to natural resources. Matt continues in the Register thanking the several Writing Program and Forest Service people who contributed to his experience. And he generously gives advice to future residents on the best two-step dancing and outdoor adventures around Taos. I was particularly impressed by his authenticity and commitment, confirmed by being the first resident to bring his own saddle.

Laura Pritchett from Ft. Collins, Colorado, was the October 2018 resident, distinguished by prior prose and drama works of fiction, as well as anthologies about conservation. A few of her sentiments:

> I am so grateful to so many—the USFS, the Leopold Foundation, the volunteers. I have read and thought much about Aldo, but it's really Estella who stays on my mind. I wonder about her life here. Yesterday my sweetie Michael and I [put] linseed oil/ mineral spirits on the deck, hoping to give back a little. This was such a gift!

Laura Paskus from Albuquerque wrote in 2019:

I've been here for the month of June and can't imagine how I'll return to life beyond Mi Casita and the Carson National Forest. My Residency…has provided the time and mental space… to finish a book project on climate change and New Mexico.… This month has also afforded me the chance to spend a ridiculous and wonderful amount of time wandering around the rocks and forests.… I've appreciated re-reading some Leopold and exploring the books from previous residents. Writing at the dining room table in the mornings and evenings, I've felt all their inspiration. Advice for future residents and visitors: never miss a sunrise or sunset, explore as far as possible into the forest, and spend a lot of time looking at the stars.

This entry was also signed by daughter Lillie Lawrence, 13, "dragged along." On the following page, Laura lists her extensive bird sightings for the month of June 2019 that I record here verbatim:

Say's phoebe, Red-winged blackbird, Northern flicker, Hairy woodpecker, Black-chinned hummingbird, Spotted towhee, Raven, Turkey, Mourning dove, Western bluebird, Cooper's hawk, Steller's jay, Western scrub jay, Lesser goldfinch, Black-headed grosbeak, Swainson's hawk, Evening grosbeak, Bewick's wren, Mountain bluebird, Kestrel, Dark-eyed junco, Nighthawk, House finch, Meadowlark, Violet green swallow, Pygmy nuthatch, American crow, Western tanager, Eurasian collared dove, American robin, Broad-tailed hummingbird, Western wood-pewee, Brown headed cowbird, Common poorwill, Grackle, Clark's nut cracker, Grace's warbler, Plumbeous vireo, Red-naped sapsucker, White-breasted nuthatch, Mountain chickadee, Ash-throated flycatcher, Chipping sparrow, Great horned owl.

As these bird lists were compiled in summer and fall, I was rewarded new sightings on a sunny mid-January day. A large wild turkey tom strolled across the north side, then hopped up the west rocks. And at the top of a ponderosa on the west rock pinnacle, a large redtail hawk surveyed the environs.

West Rocks

Enduring Service and More Writing Residencies

On a mid-September weekend in 2019, about a dozen members of the Albuquerque Wildlife Federation came to Mi Casita at my invitation. The President Kristina Fisher wrote:

> It was an honor to come help maintain Aldo's historic cabin! AWF was founded by Aldo in 1914 and we are proud to continue his legacy of ecological restoration.

Besides the visit honor, they participated in hanging the new National Historic Site plaque and enjoyed Officer Ricardo's elk burgers from his own hunting prowess.

Mi Casita opened herself in 2020 to Writing Program residents Priyanka Kumar from Santa Fe in August and

Emily Wortman-Wunder from Denver in October. From Priyanka's entry in the Guest Register:

> During my time here, I have delved deep into the arguments and the battles for conservation, and I have felt connected with the land, especially when I stumbled into bobcats in the area. As a writer I feel that Mi Casita is part of my heritage…. Mi Casita should always remain a place that fosters careful ecological thought; it should not be subject to any commercial considerations—it is too important an edifice, an emblem, and a historical structure.

From Emily's inscription:

> I am grateful that in a cataclysmic election season I have been granted this space to think on timeless matters, from the changing seasons to the role of wilderness, and wild things, in a late industrialist society…. A huge thank you to all who make Mi Casita possible through stewardship, scholarship, and community care.

I continue into 2021, selecting gems from the words left by thoughtful Residents Eve Bratman and Sarah Dimick.

In addition to scenarios of delightful and strenuous adventures, Eve reports:

> The native bees that nest in the holes of the back porch posts were my muses for writing about the plight of pollinators and their relationship to our own abilities to make peace with nature. Quiet nights spent reading Leopold and some of the other terrific works in the library here only added further inspiration…. I'm leaving with a full heart from the bounty of beauty, wildness, and time apart that being here has offered.

A final but not to be the last-ever resident, we hear from Sarah:

> Hello hello! I did most of my writing on the front porch, which had a beautiful view of the Sangre de Cristo range until smoke from the California and Arizona fires arrived…. As local

knowledge I picked up for future residents, Ghost Ranch is to-
tally mesmerizing.... Altitude sickness can be pretty strong at
8,000 feet... The Chili Line [Depot Café] is just great... and the
wifi is strong enough for Zoom calls... Hope you all enjoy your
stays here as much as I did. Soak up the porch and the birds!

As we progressed with planning Mi Casita improvements
and opportunities for the public, Ranger Angie Krall
shared the experience with other Forest Service staff in
early April. Debbie Cress wrote:

> Came to stay as part of Angie's women's workshop. Left feeling
> renewed and hopeful. So grateful for this place and this setting.

From Julie Anne Overton:

> What an extraordinary place! I'm honored to have been invited
> to the Aldo Leopold House for a women's weekend. The com-
> pany and the very special place exceeded my high expectations.
> With much gratitude.

Next, by Christi Bode Skeie:

> I'm not sure if I'm more captivated by the setting itself, or the
> words others are sharing in these pages. It gives me hope that
> there are so many of us on the "frontlines" of all these climat-
> ic and societal changes we're experiencing in the here and now.
> Who would have known Aldo's writings, thoughts, and ideas
> are even more fitting for the times today?
>
> I will treasure the time shared this weekend with other fierce
> women that are creating the change we need to see with such
> compassion and urgency.
>
> Conservation is about expanding the conversation and bring-
> ing more people along. The Forest needs your tears.

Beth Wald from El Rito:

> Such a joy and privilege to share this space, this land and time
> with other amazing women who are caring for the land and for-
> est and communities in the tradition of Aldo Leopold. And to
> be re-inspired by his deep thought and prescient words. Thank
> you!

And Deputy District Ranger Angie Krall:

> Re-awakened, Restored, Re-invigorated, the vibration and tenor of the Aldo Leopold space continues to teach, inspire, hold space. To my Ladies of Leopold, thank you for all the "workshopping" that will help the Forest Service share this space more widely but with deep consideration, and the Forest needs your tears, Te Vaya Bien.

Certain themes expressed here deserve my emphasis. While these students, writers, staff, and guests surely have extensive knowledge, their personal experiences at Mi Casita are prominent. Many come from environments with distractions of social, family, and professional life tasks. I perceive their feelings of wellness here, different from the existential dysphoria associated with ecological problems. The combination of active immersion and literate awareness is salutary, energizing, and productive. I am reminded of Scott Slovic's description of Barry Lopez's view:

> Nature writing is a "literature of hope" in its assumption that the elevation of consciousness may lead to wholesome political change, but this literature is also concerned, and perhaps primarily so, with interior landscapes, with the mind itself (p. 18).

Another feature of these self-reports is the diversity of people, at different levels of education, from varying social and ethnic backgrounds, who bring a range of more than human engagement. Note their forays into the natural environment of Mi Casita are not the adventures of affluent vacations or "back country" exclusivity. These latter may be more exploitive than contributory to a land ethic practice. Yes, some of the residents and visitors may be called elites from prestigious universities but nonetheless show good values in their actions. These are not people seeking esoteric attitudes.

The Inspiration Desk

I also recognize the work crews from government agencies. Around the country, organizations such as Rocky Mountain Youth Corps and the National Forest Foundation are engaging Native, Hispanic, and disadvantaged youth in skill and employment development through restoration programs. Locally, the state funded Youth Conservation Corps works with the Taos Land Trust. Recently, programs of New Mexico Wilderness Association Rangers and Archaeology Southwest Internships came to my attention. In Wisconsin, the Aldo Leopold Foundation sponsors Land Steward Fellowships. The U.S. Forest Service conducts a Citizen Science Program. I observe that affluent youth may be most deprived of authentic environmental experiences that are not just recreation and may benefit from such exposure and service opportunities. Apologies to any other worthy programs I omitted recognizing. I am thrilled to frequently see announcement of new opportunities.

The Guest Register still has many more pages waiting for writers, students, workers, volunteers, and visitors. And the Mi Casita historic eight acres is here for community companionship.

8

The Organic Library

Building the Soil

Organic has several definitions that apply to Mi Casita's book collection: relating to or derived from living matter, producing food (for thought?) without the use of chemicals, and an art genre having irregular and imperfect shapes. It has been so with the growth of the catalog. The idea of library collaboration for the Leopold Writing Program was part of early planning with the Rocky Mountain Land Library, but that idea did not progress and the Writing Program is no longer associated with that organization. When I began as free-range volunteer in 2015, I counted nineteen books on the shelves to the left of the fireplace. Early cabin descriptions describe the current living room as a library.

A small, framed poster on the wall adjacent to the shelves informs us:

The Albuquerque Wildlife Federation donated the USFS Carson District Mi Casita Library in memory of Richard Becker PhD to honor his devotion to the teachings of Aldo Leopold in a place where Leopold lived and loved New Mexico. July 2012.

As provided by the Albuquerque Wildlife Federation, in a memorial service for Dr. Becker sponsored by the Environmental Education Association of New Mexico, his widow Carol Chavez said:

> He felt very strongly that we, as citizens, must get involved and play a key role in managing and protecting our wildlife environments...Dr. Becker's favorite passage from "A Sand County Almanac" was an essay called "Thinking Like a Mountain."... In his doctoral dissertation he included a quote by Aldo Leopold that sums up a major goal of environmental education: "The object is to teach the student to see the land, to understand what he sees, and to enjoy what he understands."

The Wildlife Federation book donations are:

1. Julianne Lutz Newton. *Aldo Leopold's Odyssey.* First Island Press, 2008.
2. James McClintock. *Nature's Kindred Spirits.* University of Wisconsin Press, 1994.
3. J. Baird Callicott, editor. *Companion to A Sand County Almanac.* University of Wisconsin Press, 1987.
4. M. Dombeck, C. Wood, and J. Williams. *From Conquest to Conservation: Our Public Lands Legacy.* First Island Press, 2003.
5. Harley Shaw and Mara Weisenberger. *Twelve Hundred Miles by Horse and Burro: J. Stokely Ligon and New Mexico's First Breeding Bird Survey.* University of Arizona Press, 2011. Signed by the authors.
6. Richard Knight and Suzanne Riedel. *Aldo Leopold and the Ecological Conscience.* Oxford University Press, 2002.
7. Luna Leopold, editor. *Round River, From the Journals of Aldo Leopold.* Oxford University Press, 1993.
8. Aldo Leopold. *Game Management.* University of Wisconsin Press, 1933. Paperback edition, 1986.

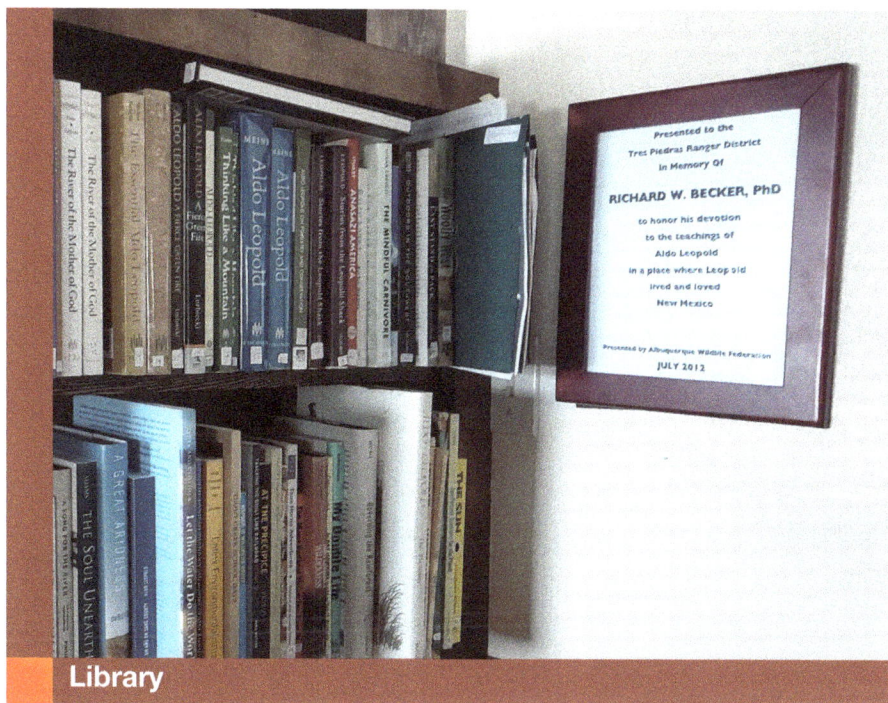

Library

9. David Brown and Neil Carmony, editors. *Aldo Leopold's Southwest*. University of New Mexico Press, 1990.

10. John Ross and Beth Ross. *Prairie Time, The Leopold Reserve Revisited*. University of Wisconsin Press, 1998.

11. Thomas Turner, editor. *Aldo Leopold: The Man and His Legacy*. The Soil and Water Conservation Society, 1995.

12. Susan Flader and J. Baird Callicott, editors. *The River of the Mother of God and Other Essays by Aldo Leopold*. University of Wisconsin Press, 1991.

13. J. Baird Callicott and Eric Freyfogle, editors. *For the Health of the Land: Aldo Leopold Essays*. First Island Press, 1999.

14. Curt Meine and Richard Knight, editors. *The Essential Aldo Leopold*. University of Wisconsin Press, 1999.

15. Marybeth Lorbiecki. *Aldo Leopold: A Fierce Green Fire*. Falcon Publishing, 2005.

16. Susan Flader. *Thinking Like a Mountain: Aldo Leopold and the Evolution of an Ecological Attitude Toward Deer, Wolves, and Forests.* University of Wisconsin Press, 1994.

Dedication and Recognition

As I became acquainted with this collection and pursued it as a syllabus for my instruction, I noticed the three more small volumes.

17. Char Miller. *Gifford Pinchot and the Making of Modern Environmentalism.* Island Press, 2001. This was inscribed by the author, "In gratitude to Ben Romero, USFS, with great thanks for an amazing visit to Taos! Char, 2/11/05."

The next two books are from unknown sources. This D.H. Lawrence collection is interesting for the essays he wrote about New Mexico when living about thirty miles east of Tres Piedras in San Cristobal intermittently from 1922 to 1925.

18. D.H. Lawrence. *The Spirit of Place: An Anthology made by Richard Aldington, Second Edition.* London Readers Union, 1944.

And someone anonymously left the paperback edition that energized the recognition of Leopold and *A Sand County Almanac* after meager initial hardcover sales of the original 1949 book.

19. Aldo Leopold. *A Sand County Almanac and Sketches Here and There.* Oxford University Press, paperback 1968.

Personal Growth

My self-assigned tutorial included investigating more literature endorsed by the Wisconsin Aldo Leopold Foundation. At this time, I was serving on the Albuquerque-based Leopold Writing Program Board and recognized the Mi Casita library's value to writer residents and visitors, as well as Forest Service staff. Program Officer Eric Garner, stationed in Questa at the time but living in Tres Piedras, noticed my interest. I realized the source of that interest. I had first read *A Sand County Almanac* in 1964 when taking likely the first ecology course taught at Princeton University. It was sophomore level, and I qualified through a high grade on the high school biology Advanced Placement test that allowed me to skip freshman biology.

An old memory emerged. I told Eric that my dual major was English and Biology, and I would have enjoyed attending graduate school in an evolving ecology program. However, the stressful and fearful circumstances of the Vietnam War draft in 1967 made medical school a safer choice for my nature. It was also the course my father preferred. His father came to America in 1895 to escape the draft imposed by the Czar for imperial expansion to the east, eventually leading to the Russo-Japanese War. The Jewish guys were often most exposed as cannon fodder. Telling this to Eric, I realized my view at the time may be offensive to the military experience of many Forest Service staff, and expressed some regret about appearing to have beens inadequately patriotic. Eric said, "You are being patriotic now." I appreciated that. At another time when he was Acting Ranger at Tres Piedras, he thanked me for my volunteer help. I quipped that I just liked to play in his yard. He said, "It is your yard too, citizen." I recently heard he is moving on to Alaska. Happy and healthy trails, amigo.

Discovering Endorsed Literature

My Wisconsin Leopold Foundation bookstore survey identified works to add:

20. Curt Meine. *Aldo Leopold: His Life and Work.* University of Wisconsin Press, 1988.

21. Jed Meunier and Curt Meine, editors. *Aldo Leopold on Forestry and Conservation: Toward a Durable Scale of Values.* The Society of American Foresters, 2017.

22. Estella Leopold. *Stories from the Leopold Shack: Sand County Revisited.* Oxford University Press, 2016.

My participation on the Leopold Writing Program Board led to more books for valuable growth. Founder Tony Anella contributed his work.

23. Anthony Anella and John B. Wright. *Saving the Ranch: Conservation Easement Design in the American West.* Island Press, 2004.

The Board included a senior scholar from the University of New Mexico School for Advanced Research.

24. David E. Stuart. *Anasazi America.* University of New Mexico Press, 2000.

Following the mission of the Writing Program, the first Annual Lecture was given by Barry Lopez. I included his National Book Award work in the library and felt grateful for the read.

25. Barry Lopez. *Arctic Dreams.* Vintage Books, 2001.

The Residents' Contributions

I then recognized the wealth of books by the Writing Program (LWP) residents. I joke that some new library additions have been read only once, my first dibs fee.

26. Tovar Cerulli. *The Mindful Carnivore: A Vegetarian's Hunt for Sustenance.* Pegasus Books, 2012. LWP 2015 resident.

27. Paul Bogard. *The End of Night: Searching for Natural Darkness in an Age of Artificial Light.* Back Bay Books, 2013. LWP 2014 resident.

28. Andrew Gulliford, editor. *Outdoors in the Southwest: An Adventure Anthology.* University of Oklahoma Press, 2014. LWP 2016 resident.

29. Andrew Gulliford and Tom Wolf, editors. *The Last Stand of the Pack: Critical Edition by Arthur Carhart.* University of Colorado Press, 2017.

30. Andrew Gulliford. *The Woolly West: Colorado's Hidden History of Sheepscapes.* Texas A&M University Press, 2018.

31. Priscilla Solis Ybarra. *Writing the Goodlife: Mexican American Literature and the Environment.* University of Arizona Press, 2016. LWP 2016 resident.

32. Gavin Van Horn and John Hausdoerffer, editors. *Wildness: Relations of People and Place.* University of Chicago Press, 2017. LWP 2015 residents.

On a later visit with his University of Western Colorado students, John inscribed: "Find and fight for Wildness, everywhere."

33. Ben Goldfarb. *Eager: The Surprising Secret Life of Beavers and Why They Matter.* Chelsea Green Publishing, 2018. LWP 2017 resident.

34. Gavin Van Horn. *The Way of Coyote: Shared Journeys in the Urban Wilds.* University of Chicago Press, 2018.

The organic library grew; residents and friends began donating.

35. Curt Meine, editor. *Leopold: A Sand County Almanac & Other Writings on Ecology and Conservation.* The Library of America, 2013. Donated by Ariana Kramer, LWP 2017 resident.

36. Bonnie Harper-Lore, editor. *Vegetation Management: An Ecoregional Approach.* U.S. Department of Transportation, Federal Highway Administration, 2013. Donated and signed by the editor, LWP 2014 resident.

37. Laura Pritchett. *Sky Bridge.* Milkweed Editions, 2005. Donated by the author, LWP 2018 resident, inscribed "To the Aldo & Estella Leopold folks—thank you for a great residency, October 2018."

38. Laura Pritchett. *Great Colorado Bear Stories.* Riverbend Publishing, 2012. Donated by the author and inscribed, "To the Aldo & Estella house—For the wild!"

39. Laura Pritchett. *Stars Go Blue, a novel.* Counterpoint, 2014. Donated by the author and inscribed, "Oct. 2018, To the Aldo and Estella Leopold Foundation folks—who burn so bright."

40. Kurt Radamaker, Cindy Radamaker, Gregory Kennedy. *Arizona and New Mexico Birds.* Lone Pine Publishing, 2007. Donated by Joan Livingston, former *Taos News* managing editor who served as LWP resident speaker coordinator, 2015–17.

41. Willa Finley and Lashard Nieland. *Land of Enchantment Wildflowers.* Texas Tech University Press, 2013. Donated by Joan Livingston.

42. Cass Adams, editor. *The Soul Unearthed Through Nature: Celebrating Wildness and Spiritual Renewal.* Sentient Publications, 2002. Donated by the editor from Taos. Signed " Wild Blessings, Cass Adams."

43. Bill Zeedyk and Van Clothier. *Let the Water Do the Work: Induced Meandering, An Evolving Method for Restoring Incised Channels.* Quivira Coalition, 2009. Donated by the Albuquerque Wildlife Federation, 2018.

44. Les Joslin, editor. *Walt Perry: An Early-Day Forest Ranger in New Mexico and Oregon.* Wilderness Associates, 1999. Donated by Sheila and Carl Roberts, Perry's Tres Piedras descendants.

45. Walter Perry. *The Land of Mañana: Memories of Old Mexico.* Maverick Publications, 2017. Donated by Sheila and Carl Roberts.

46. Corabelle Schlesser and Bonnie Harper-Lore. *Trout Creek School Days: Memories of One of the Last Rural Schools.* The Wild Rose, 2017. Donated by Bonnie Harper-Lore, LWP 2014 resident.

A Poet's Respite

47. Aaron Abeyta. *Letters from the Headwaters.* Western Press Books, 2014. Donated by the author and inscribed:

> Para Mi Casita! Thank you for the shelter, for the inspiration, for the powerful presence, especially for Aldo Leopold's legacy. Much Peace, Aaron.

John Hausdoerffer, editor, added:

> Dear Mi Casita visitor, Please enjoy Aaron's Leopold tribute letter, written from this cabin, winter 2013, beginning on page 90.

I remembered seeing Aaron at a bookstore reading in Taos. Following John's advice, I read his letter to Leopold and share the last moving paragraph:

> The sun is down. The ski is pink with alpenglow. Cruces Basin is filled with snow. Your old home is quiet. On the road below your house there are people rushing south, and I am grateful to have grown into a man with white in his beard. Thank you for the intervening years between the then and the now. Thank you for the wild places my mind recalls and my heart pounds out here, this letter, from your home, on a slight hill that looks east as the day burns itself to a black that is darker than blue (p. 97).

The Library as Beneficiary

Sometime in late 2019, I received an email from Buddy Huffaker, Executive Director of the Wisconsin Aldo Leopold Foundation. He said a retired Forest Service biologist, Gerald Burton, had offered a collection of his Aldo Leopold books for their archives. But since Gerry now lived in Albuquerque, Buddy wondered if we could accommodate them at Mi Casita. Needless to say, I enthusiastically contacted Gerry. He drove up one autumn morning with a magnificent box of books. He had been around the cabin vicinity decades ago and was thrilled to see it now restored. Here is what he contributed to our growing library:

48. David Brown and Neil Carmony. *Aldo Leopold's Wilderness.* Stackpole Books, 1990.

49. Art Hawkins and Ken Blomberg. *Letters from Art: Standing Tall in the Shadow of Aldo Leopold.* Orange Hat Publishing, 2019.

50. Frances Hamerstrom. *My Double Life: Memoirs of a Naturalist.* University of Wisconsin Press, 1994.

51. Robert McCabe. *Aldo Leopold: The Professor.* Palmer Publications, 1987.

52. Paul Errington. *Muskrats and Marsh Management.* Stackpole Co. and the Wildlife Management Institute, 1961.

53. John Hubbard. *Revised Checklist of the Birds of New Mexico.* New Mexico Ornithological Society, 1978.

54. J. Stokley Ligon. *Wild Life of New Mexico: Its Conservation and Management.* State Game Commission, 1927.

Gerry also brought ten duplicates of books previously listed. One is particularly distinctive. His copy of daughter Estella's *Stories from the Leopold Shack* is signed by Estella and inscribed to Gerry.

More donations followed:

55. Philip Conners. *A Song for the River.* Cinco Puntos Press, 2018. Signed by the author: "For the Carson USFS, Memoir from a Gila Aldo Leopold Wilderness fire lookout."

56. William de Buys. *A Great Aridness: Climate Change and the Future of the American Southwest.* Oxford University Press, 2011. Signed:

    "For Richard Rubin, Best Wishes, May 2016. W. de Buys." Tony Anella gave this to me for service on the Writing Program Board.

57. Aldo Leopold. *Un Año En Sand County.* Madrid: errata naturae, 2019. Sold by the Leopold Foundation store, I felt it was needed here.

58. Sarah Wald, David Vazquez, Priscilla Solis Ybarra, Sarah Jaquette Ray, editors. *Latinx Environmentalisms: Place, Justice, and the Decolonial.* Temple University Press, 2019. Priscilla,

now faculty at the University of North Texas, was LWP resident in 2016.

William Nordhaus, Albuquerque native and winner of the Nobel Prize in Economics, was due to be the 2020 Leopold Writing Program Annual Lecturer. In preparation, I added his recent popular book to the library, but Covid has forced postponement of the lecture.

59. William Nordhaus. *The Climate Casino: Risk, Uncertainty, and Economics for a Warming World.* Yale University Press, 2013.

Another distinguished professor, in this case of global environmental politics at American University, Paul Wapner has been a part of the Taos community for several years, conducting contemplative environmental practice retreats at the Lama Foundation. I have attended twice and included his latest succinct, thoughtful book in the library.

60. Paul Wapner. *Is Wildness Over?* Polity Press, 2020.

Another recent collection of potent thinking came along.

61. *Orion Magazine*, editor. *The Most Radical Thing You Can Do: The Best Political Essays. Orion Magazine,* 2020.

Local history and culture continued to inform and nourish us. I added:

62. Mike Butler. *Tracking the Chili Line Railroad to Santa Fe.* Arcadia Publishing, 2020.

63. Richard and Annette Rubin. *Taos Horno Adventures: A Multicultural Culinary Memoir Informed by History and Horticulture.* Nighthawk Press, 2020. We included recipes for Estella Leopold's Cornbread and Leopold Family Sourdough Pancakes as provided by the Leopold Foundation Archives.

Next, the Writing Program residents produced additions.

64. Laura Paskus. *At the Precipice: New Mexico's Changing Climate.* University of New Mexico Press, 2020. She was a 2019 resident.

65. Priyanka Kumar. *Take Wing and Fly Here.* Sherman Asher Publishing, 2013. This was a work prior to her 2020 residency.

66. Emily Wortman-Wunder. *Not a Thing to Comfort You.* University of Iowa Press, 2019. A 2020 resident, she inscribed: "Thank you to the Leopold Foundation and the Forest Service for keeping the legacy alive, Emily."

67. Eve Bratman. *Governing the Rainforest: Sustainable Development Politics in the Brazilian Amazon.* Oxford University Press, 2019. This was her substantial work which preceded the 2021 residency. She inscribed it for the library:

   To the Aldo and Estella Leopold House, with every hope for a greater future through action, thoughtful exchange of ideas, and great writing, Eve B, 6/24/21.

More from local authors to inform visitors and students:

68. Steve Tapia. *Oikos: Ecology of Northern New Mexico.* Nighthawk Press, 2016. Retired USFS and USFW naturalist from Taos.

69. Richard and Annette Rubin. *Homescape Rewilding: Stories of Ordinary Ecological Practices.* Nighthawk Press, 2021.

While scouting for new works by prior Writing Program residents, I discovered and donated:

70. Courtney White. *The Age of Consequences: A Chronicle of Concern and Hope.* Counterpoint Press, 2015. He was the first resident in 2012.

71. Courtney White. *Two Percent Solutions for the Planet.* Chelsea Green Publishing, 2015.

Enjoying our conversation about the library, Courtney said he had written a murder mystery based in Northern New Mexico. He sent a copy inscribed:

   To my fellow Leopold Residents, Happy Reading and Welcome to Northern New Mexico, Courtney.

72. Courtney White. *The Sun: A Mystery, The Sun Ranch Saga, Book 1.* Early Hour Press, 2018.

Contacting Curt Meine, Leopold's biographer, to research the *Mia* versus *Mi* Casita question, I sent him the library catalog list. He was pleased to see it and sent me four more contributions.

73. Curt Meine. *Correction Lines: Essays on Land, Leopold, and Conservation.* Island Press, 2004. Inscribed:

> To all those who keep Faith with the spirit of the land, under the roof of Mi Casita, 1-7-2022.

74. Thomas Tanner, editor. *Aldo Leopold: The Man and His Legacy.* Soil and Water Conservation Society, 2012 edition. Inscribed from Curt: "Thanks for all your efforts, Richard."

75. Larry A. Nielsen. *Nature's Allies: Eight Conservationists Who Changed Our World.* Island Press, 2017.

In his Foreword, Curt writes:

> What I especially appreciate about this book is the opportunity it provides for young people to learn a bit more about those who came before, who challenged the status quo and made changes happen. Like democracy and justice—tied, in fact, to them—conservation involves continual struggle, regular setbacks, steady advances, and occasional leaps forward. (p. xiii)

In his Introduction, Nielsen explains:

> I have chosen to stick closer to the actual practice of the field-people who rode the trails, dug the holes, and planted the trees on their way to making a national or international impact…. I see that three common characteristics flow through each of their lives: passion, persistence, and partnerships.

Next, a treasure:

76. Aldo Leopold. *A Sand County Almanac with Essays on Conservation.* Large hardcover edition with photographs by Michael Sewell. Oxford University Press, 2001. Donated by Curt Meine, with my gratitude. Inscribed:

> On your 80th birthday, dear Evelyn—with affection and appreciation and for bringing to us your wonderful son, Curt, who

has become a dear and wonderful friend and colleague. Nina
Leopold Bradley 4-27-06

On establishing the Friends of Mi Casita volunteer group,
we made more donations.

77. Robin Wall Kimmerer. *Braiding Sweetgrass.* Milkweed Editions, 2013.
78. Gavin Van Horn, Robin Wall Kimmerer, John Hausdoerffer,
editors. *Kinship: Belonging in a World of Relations, Volume 1,
Planet.* Center for Humans and Nature Press, 2021.

John inscribed on a 2022 visit to Mi Casita:

Thank you for kinning with our wild planetary family.

The day we finalized the Friends of Mi Casita Community Impact Fund at the Taos Community Foundation,
Buddy Huffaker messaged me that he received a donation in memory of Dr. Harold K. Steen of Las Cruces.
It was dedicated by the donors Don and Pat Neidig "to
the maintenance and upgrade of the Aldo Leopold cabin
in Tres Piedras." I instructed Buddy how to pass it on to
the Community Foundation and took the opportunity to
add Dr. Steen's most recent book to the library, inscribed
in his honor. I sent a note informing his widow, Mildred
Evaskovich. Three weeks later, she sent me a gracious re-
sponse and included an article she wrote about Dr. Steen.
It informs us about his career with the U.S. Forest Service,
then as faculty with the Forest History Society at University of California Santa Cruz, and later at Duke University. He was instrumental in starting the *Environmental
History Journal* and had distinguished service with the In-
ternational Union of Forestry Research Organization.

79. Harold K. Steen. *The U.S. Forest Service: A History, Centennial
edition.* University of Washington Press, 2004.

Found next in the Leopold Foundation store:

80. Stephen A. Laubach. *Living A Land Ethic: A History of Cooperative Conservation on the Leopold Memorial Reserve.* The University of Wisconsin Press, 2014.

From a new Taos Friend of Mi Casita, James Munch:

81. Eric Rutkow. *American Canopy: Trees, Forests, and the Making of a Nation.* Scribner, 2012.

Then I continued the *Kinship, Belonging in a World of Relations* series edited by Gavin Van Horn, Robin Wall Kimmerer, and John Hausdoerffer (number 78 in this list). During a 2022 visit with his students, John gladly inscribed messages to readers and writers:

82. *Volume 2: Place.* John said: "What is the place of your human and more-than-human kin?"

83. *Volume 3: Partners.* John proposed: "Here's to seeing kinship in all beings, systems, and communities as partners."

84. *Volume 4: Persons.* John's wise words: "If anything pursues its own good in its own way, then is anything not kin?"

85. *Volume 5: Practice.* John explained: "Making kin into practice of connecting with the source of all systems."

Phyllis Hotch was an honored and appreciated teacher, poet, and President of SOMOS, the Taos Society of the Muse of the Southwest. Her daughter wished the literary community to inherit the books in her extensive library. These contributions to Mi Casita were facilitated by Ariana Kramer, Leopold Writing Program resident in 2017.

86. Paul Feroe, editor. *Silent Voices: Recent American Poems on Nature.* Ally Press, 1978.

87. Annie Dillard. *Tickets for a Prayer Wheel.* Bantam Books, 1975.

While perusing the many books offered from Phyllis's library, I noticed this small one by Diné poet Luci Tapahonso. Annette and I have open hearts to Navajo culture since meeting in Chinle during medical and educational service projects after college. The book is inscribed:

Phyllis, Thanks for your support in the spirit of good stories, old songs, and the land. Luci Tapahonso, Oct 16, 1992, Taos

88. Luci Tapahonso. *A Breeze Swept Through.* West End Press, 1987.

Courtney White alerted me to a new compendium that speaks to me as an old clinical research doctor seeking to apply new ideas to practices. That warranted providing the library a copy. They also provide a newsletter service as Project Regeneration.

89. Paul Hawken. *Regeneration: Ending the Climate Crisis in One Generation.* Penguin Books, 2021.

At about book fifty, the two shelves were full, so I added a third, carefully conforming to the historic style. Carpenter Louis observed room for another. Given Forest Service plans for opening Mi Casita to public access (including a national rental program) I have wondered about appropriate protection for the collection balanced with access for educational opportunity. The original Albuquerque Wildlife Federation donation was dedicated for use by Forest Service staff. After the Leopold Writing Program began residencies, I asked the President Kristina Fisher her advice, and she reported their books were given in the spirit of free community education. To foster the catalog as a resource, I offer the list to visitors and update it conscientiously. Possibly we will obtain a cabinet in Craftsman style to secure the treasures with regulated access only. And I like the idea of leaving the donated duplicates for open benefit. We can possibly make available a copy of *A Sand County Almanac* to paying visitors. There is a paperback fiftieth anniversary edition with an excellent new

Introduction by Barbara Kingsolver, available through the Wisconsin Leopold Foundation bookstore. I think Professor Aldo would approve of that.

9

Land Preservation, Restoration, and Regeneration

As quoted by Curt Meine in *Correction Lines:*

> Kenneth Brower, introducing a new edition of Leopold's "A Sand County Almanac" in 2001, predicted that "the century or two of the Preservation Era will prove to be a prologue, an introductory chapter, noble but brief. Almost all the wilderness that can be saved has been saved. For the duration of our time on the planet—for whatever piece of eternity we have left here—restoration will be the great task."

Preservation and restoration are foundation themes in my *Living the Leopolds' Mi Casita Ecology* narrative. Leopold began as a wilderness preservation pioneer, then progressed to human restoration craft. He led his family in converting an old chicken coop into a center for their life on the worn-out Sand County farm. His devotion progressed to recovery of the damaged land. This motivation began with his early work on erosion in the Southwest. Through his scientific attitude and practices, he could expand interventions to the relationships with human practices and environmental consequences. After identifying the need for land health, Leopold's restoration at the Shack extended to the trees, prairie, and wildlife with comprehensive ecological benefits. Far too late in the damage from humans for preservation as wilderness, as Brower alludes, this land needed environmental restoration. It is now being preserved again, but differently, as an active site of ecological dynamics, scientific study, and education of people—the Leopold Memorial Reserve. In his 2014 *Living a Land Ethic: A History of Cooperative Conservation on the Leopold Memorial Reserve,* Stephen A. Laubach states:

> Following its initial introduction to the world as the central setting for *A Sand County Almanac,* the land that now composes the Leopold Memorial Reserve has served as a source of inspiration for those who seek an improved human relationship to the Earth (p. 104).

We too begin our stories with restoration of human craft at Mi Casita. Yet this cabin restoration has gone beyond the physical structure to inspire creative environmental initiatives. Historic restoration and preservation are established functions of the New Mexico Department of Cultural Affairs. The website nm.shpo@state.nm.us describes that a recognized property needs to be old enough for historic consideration, generally at least fifty years old, and that it still looks much the way it was in the past. In addition, the property must be:

- associated with events, activities, or developments that were important in the past; or
- associated with the lives of people who were important in the past; or

- significant in the areas of architectural history, landscape history, or engineering; or
- have the potential to yield information through archaeological investigation that would answer questions about our past.

Beyond the technical and administrative aspects of historic restoration, we recognize the educational, aesthetic, and inspirational qualities of this as an active process, an idea of cultural and environmental value. I think Leopold would add, it is a matter of ethics. By cultural, I mean the products and practices of human society. By environmental, I mean the entire ecosphere. And we see these as combined and integrated, not separate. Humans are within nature.

From Wilderness Preservation to Restoration

In *Two Percent Solutions for the Planet,* Courtney White teaches us about restoration agriculture, inspired by Leopold's *Biotic View of Land.* Once we can accomplish restoration, we have the duty of preservation. This is not static museum protection, but rather maintenance in natural state and vitality. And this does not seek a fixed outcome but allows the dynamic forces of evolution to continue.

Leopold often described efforts to improve the land's health. An example came to me recently from membership in Archaeology Southwest. In a recent web newsletter, www.info@archaeologysouthwest.org, Director William Doelle articulated:

> In the new year, we look forward to deepening our commitment to Preservation Archaeology.... Healing is part of why we are changing the name of our weekly outreach to you. From today

onward we are Preservation Archaeology Today. Preservation
Archaeology is guided by ethics and values. And the healing of
societies and nations may well be integrally connected to the
healing of the land.

He states that one of the organization's functions is "pre-
serving and protecting archaeological sites and cultural landscapes." This brings us back to service at Mi Casita. Implementing restoration and preservation, I wonder
about their relationship to conservation. Courtney White, a
cofounder of the Quivira Coalition, provides us clarity in
his 2014 *Grass, Soil, Hope*:

> Conservation meant prudence, care, good stewardship. And
> trust as much as it meant passing laws, enforcing regulations,
> and establishing new parks. That's why I chose a quote from
> farmer and author Wendell Berry as Quivira's motto: We can-
> not save the land apart from the people; to save either, you must
> save both (Prologue, p. xiv).

Courtney focuses us more for our Mi Casita mission:

> In our rush to engineer the world—and then try to unengineer
> it when things go badly—we forget that at heart we are intuitive
> creatures, acting mostly on emotions (p. 130).

Regeneration can be defined as a body of progressive
practices that are evolving from restoration, preservation,
and conservation. For example, White describes creative
design by Craig Sponholtz working with wetlands in the
Northern New Mexico Valle Vidal Preserve:

- increase ecosystem services and productivity
- protect and expand natural moisture-storing areas
- stabilize erosion
- restore flow and infiltration
- cultivate regenerative plant communities
- harvest runoff

- transform problems into opportunities
- create solutions that are natural processes
- strive for beauty

Psychology and Ecological Practice

I am especially attracted to the last three practices. Many environmental activists, teachers, and scholars are troubled these days, and feel validated by Leopold's observation:

> One of the penalties of an ecological education is that one lives alone in a world of wounds.

I interpret the statement as referring to the wounds of the land. Yet many commentators currently see these wounds as trauma to people. Some try to address the environmental fear, despair, grief, and pessimism heard from their readers and students. I perceive that some activists and academics feel their work has failed and express bitterness. The term *solastalgia* has been coined for the distress caused by environmental change.

Extensive commentary has developed around psychological treatment of dysphoria induced by climate change. Scientific psychology studies have examined related dynamics. However, excessive generalization of psychological phenomena may ignore the differences among people in their vulnerabilities and strengths. Much current psychological and psychiatric knowledge is applicable to this human distress and dysfunction. Subjective symptoms may not be disorder.

Rejecting the *clinical* diagnoses of our environmental angst, I see the fear, worry, grief, trauma as *existential,* meaning grounded in all human and undoubtedly more-than-human species' experience of life. Taos counselor Ted Wiard calls this "collective grief." As a trained and certified mental health science specialist and teacher, I urge responsible distinction between true clinical disorders and the conditions that are part of adverse situations in life. And yes, they may coexist in an individual. Informed evaluation is necessary for accurate and humane intervention.

Experienced mental health practitioners know that people often express their clinical disorders in the current language and issues of their time. The thoughts and emotions around environmental problems may be part of an underlying clinical disorder's pathological process. Knowledgeable assessment of impairment is a more valid reason for intervention than subjective symptoms. Anxiety may have realistic signal value, not necessarily a disorder. Grief is a normal human experience in the flux of life, and is pathological only when it is complicated by trauma harm or combined with major depressive disorder.

Some pedagogues go so far as practicing psychological counseling for these "wounds." However, they may have neglected the training vital in clinical psychology/psychotherapy to recognize the boundaries between one's own issues and those of patients, clients, students, and the diverse public. And informed consent is always ethically necessary for any intervention.

Seeking Depth

We can read more deeply for the personal Leopold. I attribute his reference to living alone as his awareness of being a pioneer scholar. Meine in *Correction Lines* writes:

On occasion, Leopold hinted at the personal cost of being eco-
logically literate, at the sadness that came with "living alone in
a world of wounds." Yet he was not by nature a pessimist or
cynic. It was always his style to realistically assess a situation,
weigh options, make the best-informed choice, and press for-
ward (p. 113).

Leopold, although acutely aware of global conservation di-
lemmas, avoided the mire of despair. One of his most notable
character traits was his capacity to face difficult conservation
problems squarely, and to address them constructively despite
overwhelming odds. This trait marked his literary endeavors as
well, and never more so than in completing "The Land Ethic"
(p. 181).

Again quoted by Meine, a postmortem review of *A Sand
County Almanac* by Louis Gannett in the *New York Her-
ald Tribune* said:

This was a man who wrote sparsely, out of intense feeling and
long experience, … Aldo Leopold was primarily concerned
with the importance of feeling something. He himself felt
deeply, and his feeling gives a rich texture to this too-short
book (p. 167).

I see psychological labeling of sensitive humans' experience as a slippery slope that may preoccupy people with
the problems to the detriment of seeking their own solutions, even in small ways. Excessive attention to being
"wounded" may leave people feeling as helpless victims.
Psychological interventions should not be mixed with social justice activism. Authorities such as police and profes-
sors need awareness of their possible confirmation bias,
projecting their own views rather than the thoughtful dif-
ferential diagnosis evaluations by trained mental health
professionals. One common situation we do abhor is the
actual physical harm and trauma caused by environmental injustice, such as exploiting homesite areas of the poor

with polluting industries, farm pesticides, and fracking damage.

Developmental psychologists have studied and debated the polarities of active and passive. These concepts have been applied also to education. Even if valid grief and trauma are suffered, I see value in shifting from more passive practices to active mastery. I will bring the issue back into the context of Mi Casita and our opportunities there. Yes, as in transforming problems into opportunities. We are progressing from the more solitary pioneering of Leopold to providing more opportunities for developing a community of like-minded activists and scholars.

Active versus Passive Conduct

Rather than viewing environmental problems as causing human "dis-ease," we can encourage, as Leopold did, attention to the health of an ecosystem as ethical practice. The Leopold Writing Program, particularly the student essay contest, offers an example of opportunity for such psychological strengthening, instead of despair. The 2022 contest (www.leopoldwritingprogram.org) provided a topic from *A Sand County Almanac:*

> Land, then, is not merely soil; it is a fountain of energy flowing through a circuit of soils, plants, and animals.... When a change occurs in one part of the circuit, many other parts must adjust themselves to it.

The contest directions then provided an essay prompt:

> What *actions* have you taken to help "tend the land" (such as protecting soil, plants, animals, wildlife habitat, water sources, etc.), or what are your *ideas* for how you and other young people can help counteract the impacts of climate disruption on the different elements of your local environment?

The Leopold Education Project

The Aldo Leopold Foundation provides a school curriculum with similar goals, available on their website www.aldoleopold.org:

- To share Aldo Leopold's land ethic, his legacy, and his writings with educators, students, and families.
- To instill in learners, through direct experience, an appreciation and respect of the natural world so they may develop a positive relationship with the land.
- To advance learners' scientific understanding of the land community's natural processes so that they may make informed decisions about conservation and land use issues.
- To advance learners' critical thinking skills through hands-on/minds-on activities.

Human Sources of Environmental Destruction

Leading Leopold scholar J. Baird Callicott poignantly summarized *A Sand County Almanac* in "The worldview concept and Aldo Leopold's project of worldview remediation" in the *Journal for the Study of Religion, Nature, and Culture,* 5: 513–532:

> From the first page to the last, Leopold aims at worldview remediation. He essays to supplant a toxic mix of biblical human exceptionalism and consumerism with an evolutionary-ecological way of conceiving and experiencing ourselves in relation to the world we share with "our fellow voyagers … in the odyssey of evolution" (Leopold 1949, p. 109).

I discussed similar thoughts in our 2021 *Homescape Rewilding* book as an essay, "Wrestling with Abraham," that parses the biblical source of humans' "dominion over the earth" (Genesis 1:26). Leopold's statement in the Foreword has become an environmental activist mantra:

> We abuse land because we regard it as a commodity belonging to us. When we see land as a community to which we belong, we may begin to use it with love and respect (p. xviii).

Inspiring, but the immediately prior sentence is rarely quoted: "Conservation is getting nowhere because it is incompatible with our Abrahamic concept of land (p. xviii)."

Essentially, as interpreted by Leopold, the prophets of three major world religions—Judaism, Christianity, and Islam—have enabled environmental exploitation and destruction. My study of this view, from Leopold's biography to various modern interpretations and responses, concludes that idea is a sociologic observation. Religious leaders seeking environmental repair and change in human conduct often cite other biblical passages that promote caretaking and moderation. Leopold himself quoted Ezekiel and Isaiah. I have learned from modern rabbinic scholars wrestling with the "dominion" controversy that the Genesis Hebrew word can be translated as "immersion." This brings us closer to Leopold's concept of "community." I share more thoughts on applying an immersion consciousness in the next chapter.

Deeper Study

Before the final 1948 Foreword to *A Sand County Almanac,* Leopold wrote a longer review of his life and works in a Foreword dated July 31, 1947. This was later abbreviated in the final publication, likely under the pressure of other publishers' prior rejections. I think the current omission of this version in discussions and activism has led to serious error and distortion. Reproduced in the Appendix of J. Baird Callicott's *Companion to A Sand County Almanac,* Dennis Ribbens states:

The 1948 foreword, which is much shorter than the 1947 one, elegantly summarizes the logic and organization of the book with relatively little comment about Leopold himself. The 1947 foreword explains the organization of the book only briefly, and for the most part develops the logic of the book less through exposition than through personal reflection. The 1947 foreword makes *A Sand County Almanac* seem much more the evolution and confessions of a conservationist. Through the 1947 foreword, *A Sand County Almanac* becomes a "vade mecum" [handbook or guide] on the trail of right thinking about man and land (p. 277–8).

In the second of the eight original Foreword pages, Leopold asserts:

Arts and letters, ethics and religion, law and folklore, still regard the wild things of the land either as enemies, or as food, or as dolls to be kept "for pretty." This view of the land is our inheritance from Abraham, whose foothold in the land of milk and honey was still a precarious one, but it is outmoded for us. Our foothold is precarious, not because it may slip, but because we may kill the land before we learn to use it with love and respect. Conservation is a pipedream as long as Homo sapiens is cast in the role of conqueror, and his land in the role of slave and servant. Conservation becomes possible only when man assumes the role of citizen in a community of which soils and waters, plants and animals are fellow members, each dependent on the others, and each entitled to his place in the sun (p. 282).

In the sixth page, we find the often quoted and misinterpreted first sentence, and then the more significant explanation that follows:

One of the penalties of an ecological education is that one lives alone in a world of wounds. Much of the damage inflicted on land is quite invisible to laymen. An ecologist must either harden his shell and make believe that the consequences of science are none of his business, or he must be the doctor who sees the marks of death in a community that believes itself well and does not want to be told otherwise. One sometimes envies the ignorance of those who rhapsodize about a lovely countryside in process of losing its topsoil or afflicted with some degenerative disease of its water system, fauna, or flora (p. 286).

The more cogent explanation is that Leopold expresses "empathy" for the land's wounds and the effects on ecologists. His judgment is not that humans are traumatized, but that many have been arrogant and have institutionalized these attitudes in fundamental belief systems. As we move from Leopold's time, about eighty years ago, to now, recognizing our responsibility for action is more urgent.

The Complexity of Stewardship

This brings us to the popularity of stewardship as the right human role. Going beyond the need to stop doing harm (the Hippocratic *primum non nocere* in my medical tradition—"first do no harm"), we are encouraged to be active in fixing environmental problems. By no means do I denigrate science and politics for contributions to environmental work and advocacy. Stewardship promotes good actions yet needs self-awareness. In applying our agency of caretaking, as stewardship is defined, we may continue to impose the fallacy that humans know better than the world's complex ecological relationships. Hmm, intellectual dominion? Stewardship should not be a cliché attitude one can superficially wear. From my medical career, I equate this ethic with practicing mutual respect and understanding by doctor and patient.

One consequence of this awareness has been recognition of the wisdom in other spiritual and religious views, as in seeking humility with the Land. Courtney White in *The Age of Consequences* asserts:

> While the toolbox of progressive stewardship is now well devel-
> oped, a great deal of our land is still in poor condition, requir-
> ing restoration and remediation (p. 205).

He later adds farmer and teacher Wendell Berry's broad definition of agrarian, calling it a way of thought based on land—a set of practices and attitudes, a loyalty and passion (p. 254). Similarly, Paul Kingsnorth in *Confessions of a Recovering Environmentalist* includes in his personal practices:

> Withdraw periodically so you can allow yourself to sit back quietly and feel, intuit, work out what is right for you, and what Nature might need from you.

Preservation for the Present, Regeneration for the Future

The legacy qualities of Mi Casita serve the values of pres-
ervation. We are glad for the institutional support of the New Mexico State Department of Cultural Affairs and the U.S. Forest Service. I recognize the methods of preservation as maintaining the important structure and setting of the eight-acre Old Tres Piedras Administrative Site. Yet, this is not a museum of artifacts to passively observe.

The concept of regeneration expresses the active evolution of environmental and human practices. Some of this work is repair, as Leopold articulated, of land health. Much has been written about current approaches. I refer you to Paul Hawken's comprehensive 2021 *Regeneration: Ending the Climate Crisis in One Generation.* Seeking personal rele-
vance, I recall now the words of the students, volunteers, and writers' expressions in the Guest Register. The cabin Library adds another dimension of experience. Someone recently posted on Facebook anonymously:

> Libraries are life raft festivals, hospitals of the soul, theme parks of the imagination, and cathedrals of the mind.

Regeneration is also a goal of the Leopold Writing Program, as articulated in the goals and mission statement described in an earlier chapter. I would like to integrate the mental health issues discussed in this chapter with the writing initiatives. Founder Anthony Anella states in the *El Piñón* newsletter (www.leopoldwritingprogram.org):

> By nurturing environmental writing, the Leopold Writing Program is making a contribution to the critically important cultural conversation about how to heal the land.

I offer that in addition, the emotional health of contemporary humans is being enhanced, both youth and adults. Resilience and constructive creativity are not new human skills. One concept to help these complex needs is recognition that the existential problems require adaptation rather than specific amelioration techniques. I view the LWP youth essay contest as providing such benefit. Regeneration also extends beyond descriptive prose writing into creative realms of art such as poetry.

Similarly, writing can go beyond the technical, scientific, and political to the idea of nurturing hope. Courtney White attempts this in his 2014 *Grass, Soil, Hope: A Journey through Carbon Country.* In addition to the beneficial influence of pragmatic initiatives, we can characterize the process of continuing efforts in the face of difficult dynamics. Eve Bratman invokes the attitude of *embroilment,* derived from the French "muddling through" as a way to be involved and resilient.

Ecological Disablement

While I recognize that restoring land health is a necessary goal, I agree with Sunaura Taylor's writing in the Winter 2021 edition of *Orion* magazine that we are in an "Age of Disability" and sometimes should recognize the need for "living well with impaired landscapes."

> Treating environmental harm and its multifaceted effects on the health of humans, animals, and ecosystems is a long-term, enduring, and at times incurable process. It is a reminder that for many ecosystems, creatures, and people on this planet, the coming decades of environmental crises will stretch not only toward death or health, but also something else—something impaired, precarious, dependent, filled with loss and struggle, requiring assistance, accommodation, and creative forms of care (p. 16).

She goes on to recognize that Leopold's concept of land health understood health as the capacity of the land for self-renewal. Disabled ecology may extend beyond Leopold's consideration of land as community to a Native/Indigenous relationship with land as family that can be maimed and made ill. My own experience as parent of a son with developmental disabilities finds this view valid, given the facts of our advancing science and changing environmental circumstances in the eighty-four years since Leopold wrote. Taylor adds:

> I want to identify disabled ecologies, and recognize our environments as disabled, not because I believe that medicalizing and diagnosing is the answer to environmental harm, but because such naming can provoke a crucial ethical attunement. (p. 21)

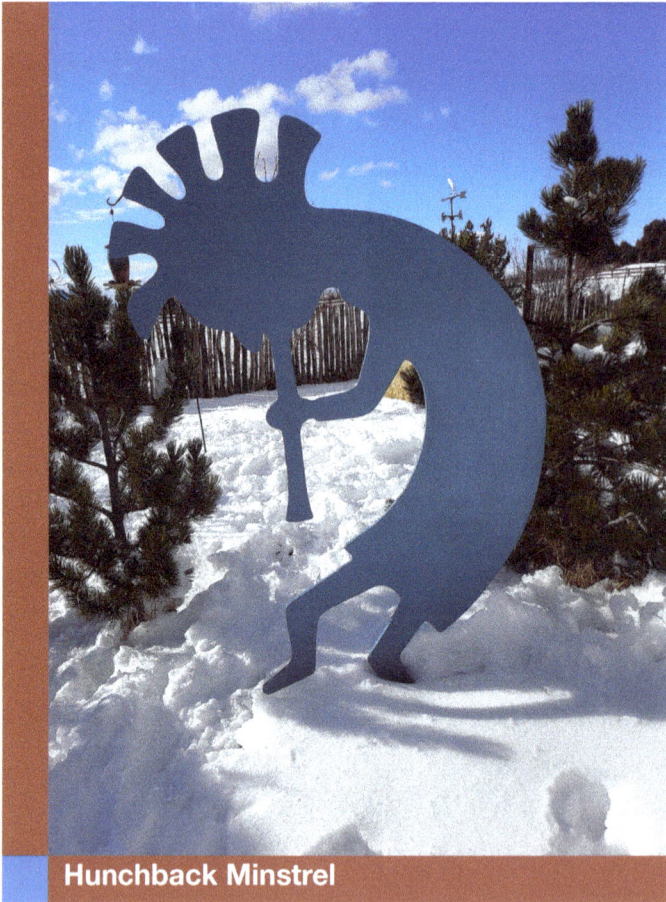

Hunchback Minstrel

This is another dimension of sensitivity to environmental justice. Annette and I know both the hardship and the spirit of life in people with disabilities from our son Brady.

Ongoing Immersion

So far in this journey, we have recognized wilderness preservation, appreciated land restoration, committed ourselves to historic preservation, and been inspired by ecological and ethical regeneration. How do we proceed with constructive intent? The U.S. Forest Service articulates how Mi Casita's value can contribute. The 2021 Revised Management Plan states:

> The final Plan provides guidance for managing the national forest to best meet the current and future needs of the American people through integrated resource management, and ecological, social, and economic sustainability.... By emphasizing multiple uses supported by healthy ecosystems and working closely with our neighbors on shared interests, the new Plan best meets the needs of the Carson National Forest and its partners now and into the future.

> The Planning Rule process:

- Strengthens the role of public participation.
- Incorporates the best available science.

- Considers a landscape-scale context for unit level management.
- Takes into account opportunities for the landscape scale resto-ration and managed wildland fire in fire adapted landscapes.
- Plan revision is an opportunity to increase public participation, and to strengthen relationships and partnerships http://www.fs.usda.gov/goto/carsonforestplan.

I wonder how a free-range citizen volunteer can participate in this mission at Mi Casita. Can we try to serve ongoing education and advocacy program development, not just maintenance tasks? Whatever we call the role, how should it be carried out, given we are attempting service within a large, complex government agency? Political lobbying and demonstrations do not serve our pragmatic local interests and relationship preferences. We wish community collab-oration attitudes. The U.S. Forest Service recognizes the value of public and private *shared stewardship*.

Developing the Friends of Mi Casita

Voluntary service and philanthropy are important meth-ods of historic restoration, preservation, and regeneration. On request of the new District Ranger, Harry McQuillen, drawing on his experience with directing a large California wildlife preserve, I looked at developing a Friends of Mi Casita group. Note I have chosen to use the familiar, less formal name. The several staff I encountered in the past few years' teamwork there were also encouraging. More interested in usefulness than publicity, I first recruited sev-eral local people with skills to share. Second, a meeting of Forest Service key personnel chaired by Ranger Ang-ie Krall produced a menu of Mi Casita priorities for the goals of improved safety and public access. With this con-fidence in our project's utility, staff developed plans to apply standard Forest Service procedures for risk assessment compliance and volunteer service. The third step was engaging a nonprofit fiscal intermediary organization that would manage our locally sourced private contributions. That is now established as a Community Impact Fund at the Taos Community Foundation for the Friends of Mi Casita. Following the charges from our new Restoration Plan, by mid-2022, the Friends have supported interior safety carpentry, installation of a protective chimney liner, and planning for fire retardant shake shingle replacement.

Implementing Ethical Stewardship

Thinking about how to describe the values expressed in this project, stewardship is often quoted as necessary for ecological service and progress. Considering the complexity of the stewardship concept, I advise distinctions where stewardship properly applies, and where our ethics should go beyond human priorities. My several years assisting with maintenance and preservation of Mi Casita are stewardship because the object is a human-made structure built by others and representing its own history. However, as friends working in a forest community, the natural vitality of the environment deserves its own recognition and respect. And there is ethical humility and integrity in recognizing the cultures that have contributed to the experience we have of these eight acres among the monumental rocks: Native American, Hispanic, Anglo-European, modern American.

While we can be enthusiastic about the celebrity of Aldo and Estella, other issues need our humble and cautious judgment in relationship with the public. While the land is National Forest, the Old Tres Piedras Administrative Site access is restricted and regulated for the safety of people and protection of the environment: natural, historic, and archaeologic. The Friends and Forest Service staff seek to practice the diligence necessary for properly expanding public participation and learning opportunities about Mi Casita's legacy.

Emulating Leopold as Teacher

Beyond his contributions to environmental science and conservation, Leopold was a teacher of university students in his later career. We can add to the depth of a Mi Casita experience by recognizing how he taught and inspired, in addition to what he wrote. Graduate student, later teaching assistant, then faculty colleague Robert A. McCabe gives us insight in *Aldo Leopold: The Professor.* He quotes him in "The Role of Wildlife in a Liberal Education," 1942:

> The objective is to teach the student to see the land, to understand what he sees, and enjoy what he understands. I say land rather than wildlife, because wildlife cannot be understood without understanding the landscape as a whole.

In "Natural History," one of the essays added to *A Sand County Almanac*, Leopold discusses education methods and criticizes technical laboratory emphasis, including required dissection of cats:

> To visualize more clearly the lopsidedness and sterility of biological education as a means of building citizens, let's go afield with some typical bright student and ask him some questions. We can safely assume he knows how plants grow and cats are put together, but let us test his comprehension of how the land is put together.

> We are driving down a country road in northern Missouri. Here is a farmstead. Look at the trees in the yard and the soil

in the field and tell us whether the original settler carved his farm out of prairie or woods. Did he eat prairie chicken or wild turkey for his Thanksgiving? What plants grew here originally which do not grow here now? Why did they disappear? What did the prairie plants have to do with creating the corn-yielding capacity of this soil? Why does this soil erode now but not then? (p. 208).

Flader and Callicott, editors of *The River of the Mother of God and Other Essays*, comment that Leopold's 1947 definition of his undergraduate wildlife ecology course objectives is one of the most succinct and characteristic statements of his role as a teacher. Published as "Wherefore Wildlife Ecology," it concludes:

> I am trying to teach you that this alphabet of "natural objects" (soils and rivers, birds and beasts) spells out a story, which he who runs may read—if he knows how. Once you learn to read the land, I have no fear of what you will do to it, or with it. And I know many pleasant things it will do to you.

Marybeth Lorbiecki adds in the biography *Aldo Leopold: A Fierce Green Fire* this quote from another of his graduate students:

> Leopold's students learned more than wildlife; they found a personal role model in their professor, a well-esteemed professional who valued his family and "kindness" (p. 148).

I had an opportunity to emulate his teaching method when John Hausdoerffer brought a group of students for a Mi Casita visit. My carpenter friend and I had been working around the cabin over several days, and one morning I found an usual scat beside the cabin. It was larger than that of the familiar coyote and my canine sidekick, and more formed than bear mounds. Hair was evident, indicating a large predator. I was uncertain of the source and sent a picture to experienced outdoorsman Officer Ricardo Leon. He gave an answer from the Eastside Forest Service biologist that was credible because the animal had been seen several times around the cabin in recent years. So I gathered the student group around and asked them to study it. I also asked them to consider how they would respond to the presence of this more-than-human community member around Mi Casita if they were living here. We had suggestions of mountain lion and wolf: possible, but unlikely and not the known neighbor. In the end, the animal was identified as a large bobcat by both the biologist (scat identification) and sightings. I left them still thinking about their relationship conundrum—and considering what the bobcat might be doing now, telling us, and needing from us by displaying this unusual behavior.

Guru Philosopher?

McCabe writes:

> Some of A.L.'s students felt that he should have assumed the mantle of guru and discussed his philosophy, especially the broad aspects of man's relationship to nature. But only rarely, and then only briefly, did he discuss philosophy as philosophy. It seemed to me that he reserved most discussions of the philosophical for special occasions in time and place. As a practical man, a pragmatist first and foremost, A.L. generally confined his philosophical insights to his writing, and seldom to the classroom. His students were to be trained as scientists, and if they succeeded, an appropriate philosophy would emerge and develop without his prompting (p. 58).

Leopold as Prophet?

Memorials to Leopold have extended to adulation as a prophet. The Wisconsin Shack has been called a shrine. Mi Casita can also be viewed that way. Teacher and poet Aaron Abeyta from Antonito, Colorado in his *Letters from the Headwaters,* gives reason for people to be at Mi Casita. He begins "A Letter to Leopold Upon Reading 'The River of the Mother of God'."

> Dear Aldo, The mountains to the east are the color of folds in a blue garment or the darkness of a river in winter, where blue presses up against the hilt of black, and I have come to the house you built, over 100 years ago, because I have heard that you were a prophet, not of the coming of Christ like Jeremiah and Isaiah, but a sybil of the hearts of men, a diviner of the desire folded into every human heart, whose secret is often revealed in the fire that men call progress (p. 90).

Hope, Resiliency, and Conservation Success

I find inspiration in a report from the Leopold Foundation website blog, beginning October 4, 2017, www. aldoleopold.org. University of Wisconsin Emeritus Professor and Senior Fellow in the Foundation Stan Temple authored "Sandhill Crane Redux" in three parts. The Foundation organizes viewing of the cranes' captivating premigration congregation on the Leopold Memorial Reserve. The landscape, once the location of Aldo's "Marshland Elegy," has been transformed into the site of a marshland celebration.

The technical definition of redux in ecology is the partial restoration of a species in a particular environment, distinguished from mass extinction. Excerpting the articles:

> The remarkable recovery of Midwestern sandhill cranes from the impending demise Aldo Leopold was anticipating in his 1937 essay "Marshland Elegy" is one of the great success stories of 20th-century conservation.... That overkill was driven in large part by commercial market hunting that was a thriving enterprise in the late 19th century, providing inexpensive

wild meat to growing populations of urban consumers.... An additional motivation for killing them was their taste for the small grain crops that were expanding across the landscape.... The Greater Sandhill Crane disappeared as a breeding bird from Illinois in 1890, Iowa in 1905, South Dakota in 1910, Ohio in 1926, and Indiana in 1929, and it was nearly extirpated throughout the rest of the upper Midwest. Until that is, the protection conferred by the Migratory Bird Treaty of 1916 with Canada and the Migratory Bird Treaty Act of 1918 which implemented the treaty.

But in the 1937 essay "Marshland Elegy," Leopold wasn't very confident that sandhill cranes would long survive even though they had been protected.... He and his students and colleagues surveyed the wetlands in the sand counties of central Wisconsin where some of the remaining cranes were still breeding. They reckoned there were just a few dozen cranes in Wisconsin in the 1930s.

I see an act of government stewardship in the next events:

Passage of the Migratory Bird Treaty Act was undoubtedly the critical action that averted the extirpation of Greater Sandhill Cranes in the Midwest.... Protection from hunting was the key since it was primarily overkill, rather than habitat loss, that had caused their decline.... Today, there are around 75,000 cranes in the upper Great Lakes region and over 15,000 in Wisconsin.... But a new issue has arisen: Should we allow cranes to be hunted again after a century of treating them as a protected species? Several species have recovered from past overexploitation and the science of modern wildlife management demonstrates how populations can be harvested sustainably.

After a thorough discussion of issues in hunting resumption, Temple adds an ethical view:

In the end, deciding whether to hunt sandhill cranes is probably less about "could" we hunt them safely, and more about "should" we hunt them at all.... I suspect the cranes have achieved an elevated cultural value and that this now transcends their value as a renewable resource that could be exploited.... I imagine Aldo Leopold would have been thrilled by the sandhill crane's remarkable recovery.... I also suspect he would have been heartened to see that the debate has taken on an ethical dimension.

Now when I see and hear flocks of cranes flying south along the Tusas Ridge over Mi Casita in the late fall towards their winter refuge in the mid Rio Grande bosques, I recognize with Professor Temple:

> Once on the brink of extinction, the sandhill crane is now considered a symbol of hope, resiliency, and conservation success.

Continuing Inspiration

Here is a final story that combines the power of literature, Leopold's teaching through immersion, the opportunities at Mi Casita, and my personal environmental awareness development. Recent consultation with Curt Meine, Leopold scholar and Senior Foundation Fellow, prompted his donation of books to the Mi Casita library. *Nature's Allies: Eight Conservationists Who Changed Our World* by Larry A. Nielsen was new to me. Chapter Four is devoted to Rachel Carson. While she is celebrated for *Silent Spring,* published in 1962, Nielsen tells a thoughtful and sensitive biography story of her early years and gradual transition from technical science writing to expressive environmental literature. He relates:

> After achieving her master's degree in marine biology at Johns Hopkins, and unable to afford pursuing a doctorate, Carson went to work in 1935 for the US Bureau of Fisheries (forerunner of the US Fish and Wildlife Service) as a writer for the public general audience.

> One assignment was a government brochure about marine fisheries that could be used to inform the public about the bureau's work. When her chief Elmer Higgins read the draft, he told

San Antonio Mountain and East Rocks

Carson that she had failed—she hadn't written a government brochure, she had produced "literature" (p. 101).

In addition to sending her back to writing a shorter, more direct version for the agency, Higgins encouraged her to send the original manuscript to the *Atlantic Monthly,* a leading national literary magazine. The editors were impressed with her eloquence and scientific prowess. The article's appearance was met with far-ranging praise. Soon after, she expanded the article into a book *Under the Sea Wind* which appeared in 1941. While a critical success, sales to the public were meager. After World War II, aided by a literary agent, Carson produced *The Sea Around Us.* It appeared in bookstores in 1951 and became immensely popular. Subsequently, her earlier book was rereleased in 1952 and also became a best-seller.

With both her own continuing scientific endeavors and recent popular acclaim, Rachel frequented the New England marine biology community from Rhode Island to Maine. My father was a graduate student in biochemistry at New York University in the late nineteen thirties. The Marine Biological Laboratory in Woods Hole, Massachusetts was a mecca for the New York to Boston research community. Our family spent summers there in the 1950s, in company ranging from my parents' graduate school friends to sharing the beach with Nobel Prize winners and their families.

The MBL conducted a Summer Science School for kids. My exploring tide pools and snorkeling along jetties was informed with biological knowledge and ecologic awareness. Carson's *Under the Sea Wind* and *The Sea Around Us* books were engaging to me. Their instructive influence was profoundly deepened by my authentic immersion experiences. I'm sure the teachers followed the progressive ecology methods of academic pioneers such as Louis Agassiz who founded the MBL and Leopold.

My personal library has included the 1952 edition of *Under the Sea Wind* and 1951 edition of *The Sea Around Us,* and those books have moved with me the past 65 years. On discovering Nielsen's chapter, I reread them. My commentary now is less about Carson, and more about my own consciousness reacting to her combination of literary style and exquisite scientific description. I wonder if this story is an example of what Mi Casita programs can contribute to learning, writing, literature, and immersion in the land.

I share now a personally moving, linguistically rich, and environmentally dynamic passage near the end of *Sea Wind:*

> Down beneath mile after mile of water—more than four miles in all—lay the sea bottom, covered with a soft, deep ooze that had been accumulating there through eons upon eons of time. These greatest depths of the Atlantic are carpeted with red clay, a pumicelike deposit hurled out of the earth from time to time by submarine volcanoes. Mingled with the pumice are spherules of iron and nickel that had their origin on some far-off sun and once rushed millions of miles through interstellar space, to perish in the earth's atmosphere and find their grave in the deep sea. Far up on the sides of the great bowl of the Atlantic, the bottom oozes are thick with the skeletal remains of minute sea creatures of the surface waters—the shells of starry Foraminifera*, the flintlike skeletons of Radiolaria*, and the frustules of diatoms. But before such delicate structures reach this deepest bed of the abyss, they are dissolved and made one with the sea (p. 260–61).

While this was written eighty years ago, I experience a contemporary "Being Here Now" inspiration.

---

*From the book's Glossary:

Foraminifera: one celled animals having limy shells with numerous pores through which long processes of protoplasm stream out. The effect is extremely beautiful.

Radiolaaria: one celled animals encased in a skeleton of silica which is exquisitely constructed like a star or snowflake.

Epilogue

If Ecology is a complex field of biological and environmental relationships, what 3 A.M. influence inspired me to write this epilogue? It came after the first working session with our conscientious book design editor Anne. Was a piece of the book missing? Our recently departed friend Phyllis Hotch published a small book of poems called "3 A.M." She describes that they "celebrate the sacredness of being alive, of reflecting about solitude and beauty, landscape and renewal." Even with my neuropsychiatric past expertise, I cannot explain this inspirational brain phenomenon. I sometimes have valuable reminders and new ideas come to me then.

One purpose of an Epilogue is to offer an insight about the book's title. Last week a friend wondered how I might be observing World Environment Day. I realized then that my interest was not Environmentalism, because as an "ism" that implies a belief system, dualistic views of right and wrong, us and them. Annette and I see ourselves living in many relationships: human, biological, terrestrial, evolutionary, and I add, spiritual. A contemplative environmental retreat leader once perceived me as a mystic, to my surprise. Therefore, we identify as ecologists in expressions such as this book and the associated life experiences.

As I told a friend who was surprised at my promptness when I wrote a piece she requested for her organization's newsletter, "when I get a word worm in my ear, I have to write it out." This Epilogue started on one of those frequent nocturnal events senior men have when Nature calls. Usually I stumble back into bed, but this time some dis-ease combination of sensing a piece missing from this book and knowing a new wildfire had erupted thirty miles west of our home drew my attention outdoors. We have been living for the past month in sight of the Hermit's Peak/Calf Canyon fire smoke plumes, the largest in New Mexico's history, thirty-five miles to the southeast. A new fire has been named Midnight and burns in Ranger Angie's El Rito District of the Carson National Forest fifteen miles south of Mi Casita.

The smoke at home was pungent the evening before. Intuitive Troi, my senior canine companion, chose to sleep on the guest room bed next to Annette's puppy Kaylee's crate, unusual for her. She knew the smells were not a typical olfactory poem left by some night creature. So when up, I went out of our bedroom at 3 A.M. to see how Troi was doing. And I opened the back door shade to look west, fearing I might see the glow of fire. Instead, through the smoke, I saw a very large red-orange moon setting rapidly in parallax mode. While I understand the physics of bending light rays, this symbolism in our time of ecological threat was powerful. Yes, red moons happen, such as last month's lunar eclipse. Yet this one was intensified through the fire. My Leopold Phenology calendar calls it the Strawberry Moon, not because of the color, but several Native American tribes see the wild fruit ripening now. A song played on KTAOS radio yesterday came to me, Jimmy Hendrix singing Voodoo Child: "On the night I was born, the moon turned a fiery red." Look up the long version lyrics. Mystical ecology in a way.

We cannot avoid or trivialize our ecological relationships. I shall go out to Mi Casita for this week's monitoring rounds with a heightened arousal and hope for the best. The Friends of Mi Casita just completed sponsorship of repairing the old, cracked chimney with a new metal liner. We have a roofing company studying replacement of the cedar shake shingles with fire-retardant protection. Today at home we exercised ecological hopefulness by planting corn in our Victory Garden, as I did with my father. Learning each year how to best augment the soil health, nurture the beneficial small creatures, and manage scarce water resources, we chose a sixty-two-day maturing variety. Our hope is feasting on the harvest when our grandsons visit soon. Hopefully it is good for us, good for our garden earth, and good for their future ecological consciousness.

References

Abeyta, Aaron A. *Letters from the Headwaters.* Western Press Books, 2014.

Bailey, Robert G. "In Harmony with Nature: A Pioneer Conservationist's Bungalow Home." *American Bungalow,* no. 83, Fall 2014.

Berry, Wendell. *The Unsettling of America: Culture and Agriculture.* Avon, 1977.

Berry, Wendell. *Think Little.* Counterpoint, 2019.

Boyer, Jeffrey. *The Tres Piedras Project.* Museum of New Mexico Archaeologic Notes, no. 19, 1990.

Bratman, Eve. *Governing the Rainforest: Sustainable Development Politics in the Brazilian Amazon.* Oxford University Press, 2019.

Butler, Mike. *Tracking the Chili Line Railroad to Santa Fe.* Arcadia Publishing, 2020.

Callicott, J. Baird. *A Companion to a Sand County Almanac: Interpretive and Critical Essays.* University of Wisconsin Press, 1987.

Carson, Rachel. *Under the Sea Wind, New Edition.* Oxford University Press, 1952.

Chronic, Halka. *Roadside Geology of New Mexico.* Mountain Press Publishing, 1987.

Cobos, Ruben. *A Dictionary of New Mexico and Southern Colorado Spanish.* Museum of New Mexico Press, 1983.

Flader, Susan and Callicott, J. Baird, editors. *The River of the Mother of God and Other Essays by Aldo Leopold.* The University of Wisconsin Press, 1991.

Geissler, Suzanne. *A Widening Sphere of Usefulness: Newark Academy 1774–1993.* Phoenix Publishing, 1993.

Gooch, Anthony and Angel Garcia de Paredes, editors. *Cassell's Spanish Dictionary, Revised.* Macmillan Publishing Co., 1978.

Gulliford, Andrew. *The Woolly West.* Texas A&M University Press, 2018.

Hawken, Paul. *Regeneration: Ending the Climate Crisis in One Generation.* Penguin Books, 2021.

Joslin, Les, editor. *Walt Perry: An Early-Day Forest Ranger in New Mexico and Oregon.* Wilderness Associates, 1999.

Kingsnorth, Paul. *Confessions of a Recovering Environmentalist.* Graywolf Press, 2017.

Laubach, Stephen. *Living a Land Ethic: A History of Cooperative Conservation on the Leopold Memorial Reserve.* The University of Wisconsin Press, 2014.

Least Heat Moon, William. *Blue Highways.* Little, Brown, & Co. 1982.

Leopold, Aldo. *A Sand County Almanac,* paperback edition. Oxford University Press, 1968.

Leopold, Aldo. *A Sand County Almanac with Essays on Conservation,* Hardcover Edition with photographs by Michael Sewell. Oxford University Press, 2001.

Lorbiecki, Marybeth. *Aldo Leopold: A Fierce Green Fire.* Oxford University Press, 1996.

McCabe, Robert A. *Aldo Leopold: The Professor.* Palmer Publications, 1987.

Meine, Curt. *Aldo Leopold: His Life and Work.* University of Wisconsin Press, 1988.

Meine, Curt. *Correction Lines: Essays on Land, Leopold, and Conservation.* Island Press, 2004.

Nielsen, Larry A. *Nature's Allies: Eight Conservationists Who Changed Our World.* Island Press, 2017.

Pearce, T.M. *New Mexico Place Names.* University of New Mexico Press, 1965.

Rifters. *The Great River.* Howling Dog Records, 2011.

Rubin, Richard and Annette. *Homescape Rewilding: Stories of Ordinary Ecological Practices.* Nighthawk Press, 2021.

Slovic, Scott. *Seeking Awareness in American Nature Writing.* University of Utah Press, 1992.

Thybony, Scott. *Dry Rivers and Standing Rocks: A Word Finder for the American West.* University of New Mexico Press, 2000.

Ungnade, Herbert E. *Guide to the New Mexico Mountains.* University of New Mexico Press, 1983.

U.S. Forest Service. *The Lookout Cookbook.* U.S. Forest Service, Region One, 1939.

Van Horn, Gavin, Kimmerer, Robin Wall, Hausdoerffer, John, editors. *Kinship: Belonging In A World of Relations, Vol. 1, Planet.* Center for Humans and Nature Press, 2021.

Ibid, *Vol. 2, Place.*

Ibid. *Vol. 3, Partners.*

Ibid. *Vol. 4, Persons.*

Ibid. *Vol. 5, Practice.*

Waters, Frank. *Mountain Dialogues.* Swallow Press, 1981.

Waters, Frank. *The Woman at Otowi Crossing,* Revised Edition. Swallow Press, 1987.

White, Courtney. *Grass, Soil, Hope: A Journey Through Carbon Country.* Chelsea Green Publishing, 2014.

White, Courtney. *The Age of Consequences: A Chronicle of Concern and Hope.* Counterpoint, 2015.

White, Courtney. *Two Percent Solutions for the Planet.* Chelsea Green Publishing, 2015.

www.ingramcontent.com/pod-product-compliance
Lightning Source LLC
Chambersburg PA
CBHW041220030426
42336CB00024B/3405